Learn-the-Alphabet
PUPPET PALS

by Mary Beth Spann

SCHOLASTIC
PROFESSIONAL BOOKS

NEW YORK * TORONTO * LONDON * AUCKLAND * SYDNEY

MEXICO CITY * NEW DELHI * HONG KONG * BUENOS AIRES

Dedication

To the memory of Shari Lewis, whose brilliant artistry as a puppeteer
and ventriloquist enchanted me when I was a young child, and whose
energy, spirit, and vision inspire me still.

To Jeff Peyton, founder of Puppetools, Inc., a company whose core belief is
that puppetry transforms and transcends the boundaries of traditional
education by empowering teachers and students to think, imagine,
and communicate with creativity and passion.

To Katie Polk, an enormously talented puppeteer, who knows how to play freely with
ideas and possibilities and who easily invites young people to do the same.

To the students who have enjoyed puppetry with me,
and to the teachers who courageously gave it a try.

To the best teaching assistants ever: Kerry Koala, Cookie the Frog, Bully Bullfrog,
Patti Perfect, Stinkie the Skunk, and Pinkie the Mouse. Thanks, guys.

And last but not least, with love to my family, especially my children, Francesca and James,
who served as a captive audience to many hours of Mom's puppeteering efforts.

Cover design by Gerard Fuchs
Cover and interior artwork by Rusty Fletcher
Interior design by Sandra Harris, Ampersand Design

ISBN: 0-439-13118-9
Copyright © 2003 by Mary Beth Spann
All rights reserved. Published by Scholastic Inc.
Printed in the U.S.A.

1 2 3 4 5 6 7 8 9 10   40   09 08 07 06 05 04 03

Contents

A Note from the Author

Welcome!

I am thrilled to invite you into the world of possibilities that lies ahead as you begin using puppets with your students. Learn-the-Alphabet Puppet Pals is an outgrowth of my own experience in using puppets with children. This book provides you with everything you need to teach the alphabet and letter sounds with stick puppets.

If you're new to using puppets in the classroom, this book can serve as a beginner's guide to navigate you through the preparation and instructional aspects of being a puppeteer teacher. For the veteran puppeteer, this book offers fresh and fun puppet activities that can be used and adapted to your own personal style. Inside you'll find puppet patterns, stories, and activities for each letter of the alphabet. All you need to supply is a few craft materials, a roomful of eager children, and your own enthusiasm. So grab your scissors and glue and let's get started!

-Mary Beth Spann

About This Book

For each alphabet letter, you'll find:

- A reproducible stick puppet pattern, plus complete directions for using that same basic pattern to craft simple student puppets as well as more elaborate teacher puppets.

- A Puppet Pointers section, in which directions are given for creating a more durable teacher's puppet with visual and tactile interest to children.

- A reproducible Read-Aloud Puppet Story featuring the puppet character. Each brief story is sprinkled with words beginning with the letter for the unit. You can use the story with children to explore the letter sound as well as story elements (such as theme, character, plot, and setting).

- An interactive Pocket-Chart Poem which encourages reading, rhyming, and recall skills. You can print each poem on sentence strips and then display these in a pocket chart. While reading the poem with children, you can use your puppet as a pointer. You can also use sentence-strip segments printed with new words to substitute for words in each poem, thus creating interactive rhyme alternatives. You might also give children copies of the poem to illustrate, or make multiple copies of the poem as it appears in the box on the book page and then cut and glue a poem box to the back of each stick puppet.

* The Setting the Stage section provides activities to help children step into each story by building anticipation and giving them a purpose for listening.

* The Extension Activities offer puppet movement tips and other activities to help children use their letter knowledge and listening skills. You can adapt most of these activities for use with other letter units.

* The Practice Printing gives students practice in tracing and writing the feature letter. To make these pages reusable, you might laminate them or slip them into clear plastic sleeves. Then students can practice printing the letters with wipe-off markers.

Learn-the-Alphabet Puppet Pals helps provide your young students with an imaginative, fun-filled introduction to the alphabet—one that helps foster alphabet awareness while exploring letter configurations and sound/symbol relationships. The 26 Puppet Pals are presented in alphabetical order, but feel free to use them in any order and in any way you wish. You might, for example, use them to enhance or supplement your existing alphabet program. *Puppet Pals* is comprehensive enough to serve as a core alphabet curriculum, but no matter how you put them to use, the Puppet Pals are ready to enchant and engage your students in solid alphabet learning fun.

Making the Puppets

Did you know that puppeteers are among the few performing artists who craft their own medium of expression? So the first step in teaching with puppets is crafting the puppets you'll be working with.

The patterns provided in this book are meant to help you craft student and teacher versions of each puppet model. Student puppets are made of paper and are easy for youngsters to assemble without much adult assistance. Teacher puppets are sturdier versions of the student puppets. They are fancier puppets, so they are also more visually and tactilely appealing. Once you make your set of teacher puppets, you will save and reuse them year after year.

Decorating tips (Puppet Pointers) for each teacher puppet are provided with each puppet model.

Directions for Making Children's Puppets:

You will need:

- ★ set of puppet patterns (one per each puppet)
- ★ crayons or colored pencils (preferable to markers which tend to "bleed" and can obliterate the character's details)
- ★ construction paper
- ★ craft sticks (tongue depressor size)
- ★ white craft glue
- ★ scissors

Steps:

1. Copy each puppet pattern onto copy paper. Have children color puppets as desired.

2. Cut out each puppet along dashed line. Color in as desired.

3. Place stick between puppet pattern and construction paper backing; let dry completely, then trim construction paper to match puppet shape.

4. Print children's names on the craft sticks. Children may use puppets as is, or they may glue on small details such as wiggle eyes, yarn hair, fabric bits, etc.

 Tip You may also want children to make puppets to represent the other characters in each story. To do this easily, simply glue each stick between two large unruled index cards and let children draw the characters on the cards. Trim around edges of characters, if desired.

Directions for Making Teacher Puppets:

You will need:

- ★ set of puppet patterns
- ★ discarded file folders or oaktag
- ★ assorted colors of craft foam (sold in sheets; available in craft and department stores)
- ★ craft sticks (tongue depressor size)
- ★ white craft glue
- ★ scissors
- ★ permanent fine-tip markers in black and assorted colors
- ★ assorted art trims and notions
- ★ glitter glue; puff paints (optional, but work very well on craft foam)

Steps:

1. Copy each puppet pattern onto copy paper. Trace entire pattern outline onto craft foam to serve as the puppet base. Cut apart smaller details from the large paper pattern; use these smaller pieces to trace on and cut out details from contrasting colors of craft foam. (For example, if you outline and cut out an animal puppet shape from a piece of craft foam and then wish to cut a hat for that animal, cut away the paper hat to use as a pattern, trace the hat shape on contrasting color of craft foam, then glue the foam hat to the foam base, which already includes the hat shape.)

2. Place stick between puppet pattern and paper backing; let dry completely, then trim paper to match outline of puppet shape.

3. Glue details to the puppet such as wiggle eyes, yarn hair, fabric clothes, etc.

 Tip Be sure to look for the Puppet Pointers that accompany each puppet model, as these offer fun specific design ideas for each one.

Teaching With Puppet Pals

The puppet activities in this book are straightforward and easy to use. Below are some tips for preparing to use the puppets and stories with students:

⭐ Before sharing a story, read it a few times to familiarize yourself with the vocabulary, plot, and structure.

⭐ Make a copy of each story for yourself and students. Distribute student copies after you share the story orally.

⭐ Discuss together your behavioral expectations for using the puppets. At the same time, you'll want to set a lighthearted tone for puppet interactions. One effective way to do this is to establish a practice of speaking directly to the puppets about their behavior. For example, you might compliment puppets when they remain in their own space and "pay attention." Or you might remind a puppet that it needs to either stay focused or return to its puppet container. Another strategy is to apologize to the puppeteer for a puppet's less-than-perfect behavior. ("James, I'm sorry to see your Alec Alligator puppet is having trouble sitting in your lap. Perhaps he needs to step to another part of the room for a while. Your Alec puppet can join us again later.") This insures the child will automatically "manage" the puppet better next time.

⭐ Let each puppet tell the children about the other characters they will meet in his or her story.

⭐ As you tell the story, hold your puppet so that the speaking character faces the children. Remind them to hold their puppet characters forward to face their audience (initially, you).

⭐ Tell children that as you read the story, they should listen for words that suggest movements and actions they can act out with their puppets. (Refrain from suggesting or performing these yourself. That way, children will be prompted to generate their own ideas.)

⭐ Retell the same story several times, then invite volunteers to take turns telling stories.

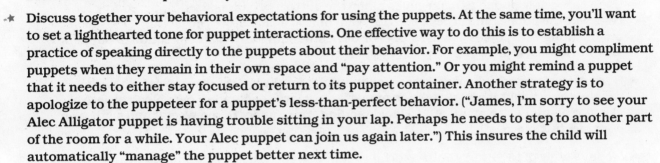

Investigating Print

The unit stories are perfect tools for investigating different print elements used in reading and writing. You might ask children to find and circle some of the following in their copies of the stories:

⭐ a specific upper- or lowercase letter

⭐ words beginning with a given letter, vowel sound, or specific sound for a given letter (such as the hard and soft sounds of *c* and *g*)

⭐ words containing a specific vowel sound, such as short *a*

⭐ target words, such as character or object names

⭐ repeated words and phrases

⭐ parts of speech, such as verbs and adjectives

⭐ synonyms and antonyms

⭐ days of the week

⭐ the capital letter at the beginning of a proper name

⭐ punctuation, such as periods and quotation marks

Tip Students may use highlighting markers, highlighting tape, crayons, pencils, or even just their fingers to locate and flag target story elements.

Storing and Displaying the Puppet Pals

Use some of these ideas for storing and displaying your puppets and stories:

* Slip a copy of each story into a loose-leaf page protector. Store the stories in a loose-leaf notebook. Also keep copies of the reproducible pages and pocket-chart poems in this notebook.

* Use a three-hole punch to make holes along the bottom of gallon-sized zippered freezer bags. Put the puppet and accessories for each unit in a bag. Store the bags in a loose-leaf binder along with copies of each story. Or have students store their collection of puppets and stories in a sturdy plastic pocket folder.

* During a letter study, display your teacher puppet for that letter in a special place. For example, you might insert your stick puppet into a large decorated foam block or into a clay pot planter (with plant). Add a label reading "Our Puppet of the Week!" and set it near your meeting place.

* Mount a copy of each story onto colorful paper or oaktag. Display the stories in alphabetical order, along with the corresponding teacher puppets, to serve as an alphabet wall border. The border can double as a reminder of the sound for each letter.

Making Home-School Connections

Reinforce students' knowledge of letters and sounds by communicating with parents about their puppet work. Here are some effective ways to make a home-school connection:

* Before beginning your exploration of the alphabet with puppets, send a parent note home to explain the program. Encourage parents to ask their children what they learned with their puppets each week. Also use your class newsletter to give puppet updates.

* Send student folders home so that children can enjoy the puppets and stories with their parents. Suggest that parents read the story while their children use their puppets to act it out.

* At the end of the school year, hold a Puppet Pal Celebration. Give parents the task of providing snacks that begin with each letter of the alphabet. (Send home a list of safe food suggestions for families to choose from.) During the celebration, have children present their completed alphabet story and puppet folders to parents.

Alec Alligator

alligator

Read-Aloud Puppet Story

Setting the Stage: Invite children to share their apple-picking experiences with the class. Then tell them that they will hear a story about an alligator who picks apples. Encourage children to think about how difficult this might be for an alligator.

Pocket-Chart Poem

Building Reading Skills: Print each line of the poem on a sentence strip. Place strips into a pocket chart. After reciting the poem several times, ask children what other words could substitute for apple pies (*apple fritters, apple muffins, apple cakes, apple cookies,* and so on). Print these variations on separate sentence-strip segments cut to fit over the original words. Have children take turns inserting the word cards into the pocket chart and then reading aloud the new versions.

Extension Activities

Stick Puppet Drama: Invite children to use their stick puppets to act out Alec's feelings and actions as they occur in the story. Afterward, have children demonstrate the different ways they moved their puppets to show some of the following: Alec baking, walking, climbing, and picking; Alec acting excited, then disappointed, about the wishes; and Alec happy to have all the apples he needs.

Read the story again so children have a chance to try out the different movements demonstrated.

Listen for Short A: Explain to children that Alec Alligator's name begins with the short sound for *a*. Say his name several times to reinforce the sound. Then have children hold their puppets in their laps as you reread the story. When they hear Alec's name—or any other word beginning with short *a*—have children draw an *a* in the air with their puppets.

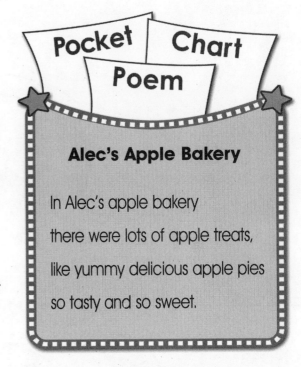

Pocket Chart Poem

Alec's Apple Bakery

In Alec's apple bakery

there were lots of apple treats,

like yummy delicious apple pies

so tasty and so sweet.

Puppet Pointers

1. Trace the alligator onto green craft foam. Cut it out. Add details with a fine-tip permanent marker.

2. Cut basket and apples, worm and hat from contrasting colors of craft foam (e.g., red for apples).

3. Glue wiggle eyes onto the alligator and worm.

4. Use silver glitter glue to add shine to apples.

Stick Puppet Pattern

Directions: Color and cut out the puppet pattern.
Glue a craft-stick handle to the back. Use the puppet
as a storytelling prop.

alligator

Aa is for Alec Alligator

Alec Alligator

alligator

Alec Alligator owned an apple bakery. Every day he baked tasty apple treats… apple pies, apple muffins, apple cookies, apple anything! But picking and carrying apples was hard work for an alligator. Alec made many trips to and from the apple tree. Often, he wished that all the apples in the world were brought right to his bakery.

One day, Alec put on his hat and left to pick apples. Soon he came to a tree filled with red, juicy apples. He put his basket down and picked an apple. Just then, a worm's head popped out of the apple. "Please don't bake my apple," begged the worm. "Leave my home alone, and I will grant you three wishes."

"Three wishes!" said Alec. "Wow! I wish that all the apples in the world were brought right to my bakery!" Suddenly, Alec was at his bakery, and he was surrounded by apples! The surprised alligator cried, "Oh, no! That's not what I really meant! I wish I never wished that wish!" At once, the apples disappeared and Alec was at the apple tree again. "Oh, my! I just wasted two wishes," cried Alec.

"What do you really want?" asked the worm. "What I really wish for," said Alec, "is to have enough apples to bake my recipes every day." "Well, why didn't you say so?" said the worm.

Since then, Alec had just enough apples to bake his recipes every day. And he always was very careful about what he wished for.

Practice Printing

alligator

Name _____

A A A A A A A A A A A A

A A

A A

a a a a a a a a a a a

a a

a a

Aa Aa Aa Aa Aa Aa Aa Aa

Aa Aa

Aa Aa

Bonny Bunny

Read-Aloud Puppet Story

Setting the Stage: Invite children to tell how they celebrate their birthdays. Then tell them that they will hear a story about a bunny birthday. Ask them to listen for ways in which this bunny celebration resembles their own birthday celebrations.

Pocket-Chart Poem

Building Reading Skills: Print each line of the poem on a sentence strip. Place strips into a pocket chart. After reciting the poem several times, ask children what other words could substitute for hopped and hopped (*played and played, jumped and jumped, sand and sang, bounced and bounced,* and so on). Print these variations on separate sentence-strip segments cut to fit over the original words. Have children take turns inserting the word cards into the pocket chart and then reading aloud the new versions.

Pocket Chart Poem

Bonny's Birthday

Bonny Bunny's special day

was filled with birthday fun.

With bracelets, bows, and a big beach ball,

she hopped and hopped till the day was done.

Extension Activities

Stick Puppet Drama: Invite children to use their stick puppets to act out Bonny's feelings and actions as they occur in the story. Afterward, have children demonstrate the different ways they moved their puppets to show Bonny imagining bouncing her ball, Bonny opening her presents, and Bonny trying on her gifts.

Read the story again so children have a chance to try out the different movements demonstrated.

Bouncing for B's: Tell children that Bonny Bunny's name begins with the sound for *b*. To help them identify this sound in the story, ask children to place their puppets and beach balls in their laps. Explain that, as you read the story, they should bounce their puppets and beach balls each time they hear a word that begins with *b*. Then, when children bounce their puppets, pause and write the identified word on your alphabet word wall or chart paper. At the end of the story, review all the *b* words with students.

1. Glue craft fur, cotton batting, or terry cloth to the bunny shape. Trim the excess material.

2. Add details with a fine-tip permanent marker.

3. Add wiggle eyes and yarn whiskers.

4. Glue ribbon bows around Bonny Bunny's ears and arms.

5. Cut a craft foam ball for Bonny to bounce.

Stick Puppet Pattern

Directions: Color and cut out the puppet pattern.
Glue a craft-stick handle to the back. Use the puppet
as a storytelling prop.

Bb is for Bonny Bunny

Bonny Bunny

Bonny Bunny's birthday was just a few days away. Bonny's family always celebrated birthdays with balloons, bunny cupcakes with little carrots on top, and beautiful boxes tied with bows. This year, Bonny hoped that one of her birthday boxes would hold a big beach ball, the kind with bright stripes of colors. A beach ball to *bounce-bounce-bounce* all around!

Finally, the big day arrived. As always, Bonny's mom brought home a bunch of balloons. Bonny's dad made his special bunny cupcakes with little carrots on top. Bonny's brother and sister surprised her with three beautiful boxes tied with bows.

Bonny opened the first box. It held two floppy ear-bows. Bonny put the bows on her ears. *Flop-flop-flop!* Then she opened the second box to find a set of bangle bracelets. Bonny put the bracelets on her arm. *Clang-Clang-clang!* Finally, she opened the last box. Inside was a flat, colorful piece of plastic with a tiny straw at one end.

"What's that?" said Bonny. Dad picked up the plastic and blew air into the straw. *Whoosh-whoosh-whoosh.* The plastic colors began to grow. *Puff-puff-puff.* The plastic was getting big and round. Surprise! Bonny's last gift was a big round beach ball with bright stripes of color.

"It's just what I wanted!" cried Bonny. The happy bunny began to *hop-hop-hop* and *bounce-bounce-bounce* her beach ball all around. At the end of the day, Bonny thanked her family for the hoppiest, bounciest birthday ever!

Practice Printing

Name

B B B B B B B B B B B B B

B B

B B

b b b b b b b b b b b b b

b b

b b

Bb Bb Bb Bb Bb Bb Bb Bb Bb

Bb Bb

Bb Bb

Calico Cat

cat

Read-Aloud Puppet Story

Setting the Stage: Invite children to share about times when they've been tired. How did they behave? Do they ever get crabby or cranky when they are tired? After sharing, tell children that they will hear a story about a tired cat who is cranky because she can't get to sleep.

Pocket-Chart Poem

Building Reading Skills: Print each line of the poem on a sentence strip. Place strips into a pocket chart. After reciting the poem several times, ask children what other words could substitute for *clang-clang-clang (clap-clap-clap, clatter-clatter-clatter,* and so on). Print these variations on separate sentence-strip segments cut to fit over the original words. Have children take turns inserting the word cards into the pocket chart and then reading aloud the new versions.

Extension Activities

Stick Puppet Drama: Invite children to use their stick puppets to act out Calico Cat's feelings and actions as they occur in the story. Afterward, have children demonstrate the different ways they moved their puppets to show Calico complaining, Calico reacting to the night sounds, and Calico feeling the comforter fall on her. (Tip: Children may use pieces of cloth or their free hands to serve as the comforter.)

Read the story again so children have a chance to try out the different movements demonstrated.

Listen for C: Tell children that the letter *c* can make two sounds: the sound of *k* (hard *c*) and the sound of *s* (soft *c*). Ask them to name the sound heard at the beginning of Calico Cat's name (hard *c*). Contrast this with the sound of soft *c* as in *city* or *circus* (or any of their classmates' names that begin with soft *c*). To provide practice in listening for the hard *c* sound, have children hold their puppets in their laps. Then name one word at a time that begins with either the hard or soft *c* sound. Ask children to raise their puppets if the word begins with a hard *c*, as in Calico Cat. After children respond with their puppets, review the word and its beginning sound.

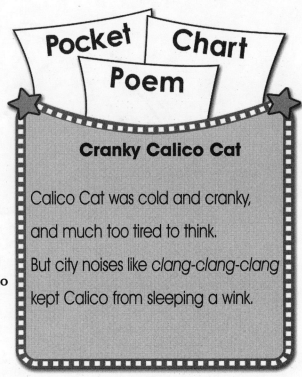

Pocket Chart Poem

Cranky Calico Cat

Calico Cat was cold and cranky,

and much too tired to think.

But city noises like *clang-clang-clang*

kept Calico from sleeping a wink.

Puppet Pointers

1. Glue craft fur or terry cloth to the cat shape. Trim the excess material.

2. Add details with a fine-tip permanent marker.

3. Add wiggle eyes and yarn whiskers.

4. Use a scrap of terry cloth, blanket fabric, or a doll's quilt as a comforter prop.

Stick Puppet Pattern

Directions: Color and cut out the puppet pattern.
Glue a craft-stick handle to the back. Use the puppet
as a storytelling prop.

cat

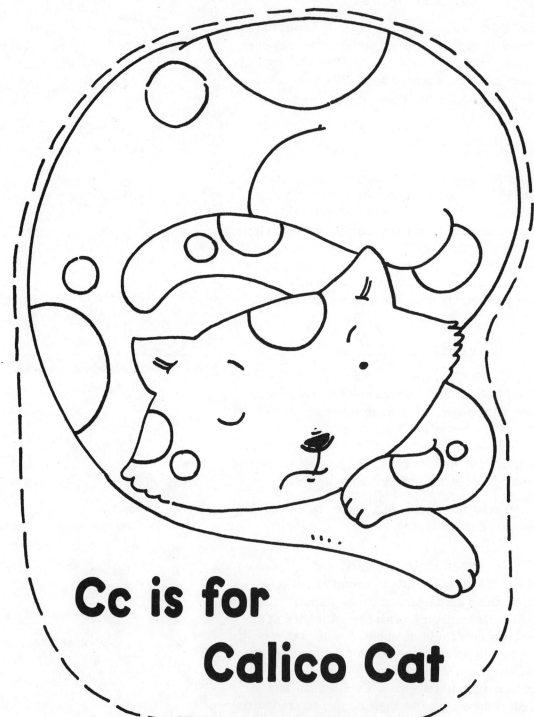

Cc is for Calico Cat

Calico Cat

Calico Cat was cranky. No matter how hard she tried, she could not get to sleep. It was cold and noisy in the alley where she tried to curl up and get comfortable. "The problem," grumbled Calico, "is that the city night is too cold and the city sounds are too loud. The noise never stops!"

Calico curled up and closed her eyes tight. She tried not to listen. First, she tried not to listen to the fire truck bell that raced down the street. *Clang-clang-clang! Clang-clang-clang! Clang-clang-clang!* The noise frustrated Calico so much that she dug her claws into the ground.

Next, she tried not to listen to the shoes that walked by on the sidewalk. *Clap-clap, clap-clap. Clap-clap, clap-clap. Clap-clap, clap-clap.* The noise frustrated Calico so much that she dug her claws into a wall.

Finally, she tried not to listen to the cars and trucks that rattled over the bumpy streets. *Clatter-clatter-clatter, clatter-clatter-clatter, clatter-clatter-clatter.* The noise frustrated Calico so much that she tried to dig her claws into the cold, loud air.

But the city sounds just got louder and louder. Frustrated Calico tipped her head back to cry. At that moment, something fell from the wall above and landed on Calico. Surprise! It was a soft, cozy comforter and it surrounded Calico with warmth . . . and silence! Wrapped in the comforter, Calico no longer felt the cold city night or heard the loud city sounds. So she relaxed her claws, curled up tight, and fell fast asleep.

Practice Printing

cat

Name

C C C C C C C C C C C C C

C C C

C C C C C C C C C C C C C

C C

C C

Cc Cc Cc Cc Cc Cc Cc Cc

Cc Cc

Cc Cc

 # Danielle Dinosaur

dinosaur

Read-Aloud Puppet Story

Setting the Stage: Ask children to share their experiences and feelings about learning how to do something new. After sharing, tell them that they will hear a story about a dinosaur who worries about learning to dance.

Pocket-Chart Poem

Building Reading Skills: Print each line of the poem on a sentence strip. Place strips into a pocket chart. After reciting the poem several times, ask children what other words could substitute for Dinosaur-Egg Dance (*Dinosaur Ice-Age Dance, Dinosaur Dipsy-Doodle,* and so on). Print these variations on separate sentence-strip segments cut to fit over the original words. Have children take turns inserting the word cards into the pocket chart and then reading aloud the new versions.

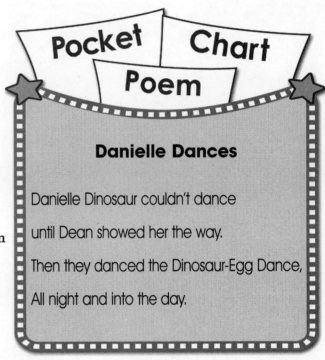

Pocket Chart Poem

Danielle Dances

Danielle Dinosaur couldn't dance

until Dean showed her the way.

Then they danced the Dinosaur-Egg Dance,

All night and into the day.

Extension Activities

Stick Puppet Drama: Invite children to use their stick puppets to act out Danielle Dinosaur's feelings and actions as they occur in the story. Afterward, have children demonstrate the different ways they moved their puppets to show Danielle feeling disappointed, Danielle dragging herself to the door, and Danielle doing the dances described.

Read the story again so children have a chance to try out the different movements demonstrated.

What's in a D Name? Tell children that Danielle Dinosaur's name begins with the sound of the letter *d*. Challenge children to brainstorm as many *d* names as possible. Invite them to search the classroom, as well as books in your class library. Record student responses on a chart or on your alphabet word wall. Guide children to understand that a proper name always begins with an uppercase letter.

Puppet Pointers

1. Trace the dinosaur onto brown, gray, or green craft foam.

2. Add details with a fine-tip permanent marker.

3. Glue on wiggle eyes.

4. Outline dinosaur with green puff paints.

5. Use glitter glue to color in dinosaur spots.

Stick Puppet Pattern

Directions: Color and cut out the puppet pattern.
Glue a craft-stick handle to the back. Use the puppet
as a storytelling prop.

dinosaur

**Dd is for
Danielle Dinosaur**

Learn-the-Alphabet Puppet Pals Scholastic Professional Books

Danielle Dinosaur

Danielle Dinosaur was disappointed. All the dinosaurs in her class had invitations to the Annual Dinosaur Dance . . . except her.

While she was feeling down, the doorbell rang. *Ding-dong!* Danielle dragged herself to the door.

"Special delivery for Danielle Dinosaur!" said Dean Dinosaur with a smile as he handed Danielle a letter. She opened the envelope and smiled. It was an invitation to the dance!

Suddenly, her smile dropped again. "Oh dear! I have an invitation now, but I forgot that I don't know how to dance," said Danielle sadly.

"I can teach you!" said Dean.

"I don't think I can learn," said Danielle.

"Of course you can. They don't call me 'Dancin' Dean' for nothing," said Dean. "I can teach any dinosaur to dance! I'll teach you, too."

The next day, Danielle's dad drove her to Dean's house for her dancing lessons. There was so much to learn! Dean showed Danielle how to curl up then jump high to "hatch" for the Dinosaur-Egg Dance. He taught her how to shake and then freeze into an iceberg for the Ice-Age Dinosaur Dance. Danielle learned how to dip to the left, right, front, and back to do the Dinosaur Dipsy-Doodle. The dinosaurs practiced their dances all day long.

On the night of the Annual Dinosaur Dance, Danielle and Dean danced until they dropped.

"Dean, I'm delighted that you taught me how to dance!" exclaimed Danielle.

"Well, I never doubted that you could learn," said Dean, as he proudly danced his way home.

 # Practice Printing

dinosaur

Name

D D D D D D D D D D D D D

D D

D D

d d d d d d d d d d d d d

d d

d d

Dd Dd Dd Dd Dd Dd Dd Dd

Dd Dd

Dd Dd

Elly Elephant

elephant

Read-Aloud Puppet Story

Setting the Stage: Discuss with children the different ways they get exercise through sports and activities that they enjoy. Point out that people can get exercise in a variety of ways. Then tell students that they will hear a story about an elephant who is looking for the best exercise for her.

Pocket-Chart Poem

Building Reading Skills: Print each line of the poem on a sentence strip. Place strips into a pocket chart. After reciting the poem several times, ask children what other words could substitute for flapped like Eagle (*jumped like Elk, shimmied like Ermine,* and so on). Print these variations on separate sentence-strip segments cut to fit over the original words. Have children take turns inserting the word cards into the pocket chart and then reading aloud the new versions.

Extension Activities

Stick Puppet Drama: Invite children to use their stick puppets to act out Elly Elephant's feelings and actions as they occur in the story. Afterward, have children demonstrate the different ways they moved their puppets to show Elly walking (slowly), Elly flapping, and Elly jumping and shimmying.

Read the story again so children have a chance to try out the different movements demonstrated.

Listen for E: Tell children that Elly Elephant's name begins with the short sound for *e.* Say her name several times to reinforce the sound. Then ask students to listen to the story for other words that begin with the short *e* sound. As you read, invite groups to take turns acting out the story with their puppets. Each time students hear a word beginning with the short *e* sound, have them hold up their puppets to signal the "actors" to freeze. Then record the identified *e* word on a chart or on your alphabet word wall. Afterward, review all the *e* words with students.

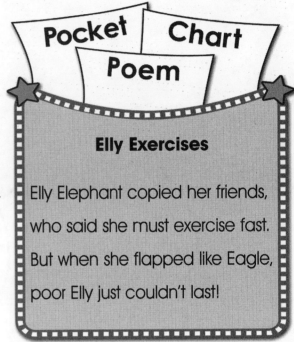

Pocket Chart Poem

Elly Exercises

Elly Elephant copied her friends,

who said she must exercise fast.

But when she flapped like Eagle,

poor Elly just couldn't last!

Puppet Pointers

1. Trace the elephant shape onto gray craft foam. Cut it out.

2. Add details with a fine-tip permanent marker.

3. Glue on wiggle eyes.

4. Glue on an artificial flower.

Stick Puppet Pattern

Directions: Color and cut out the puppet pattern.
Glue a craft-stick handle to the back. Use the puppet
as a storytelling prop.

elephant

Ee is for
Elly Elephant

Learn-the-Alphabet Puppet Pals Scholastic Professional Books

Elly Elephant

Elly Elephant always felt lots of energy when she took a walk. For exercise, she would swing her trunk and sway her body slowly as she walk-walk-walked through the grass. But her friends, Eagle, Elk, and Ermine told Elly that she should move extra fast to exercise. "Do what we do," they said. "Then you will have more energy!"

So Elly tried to exercise like Eagle. She watched Eagle spread her wings and flap-flap-flap extra fast to soar over the trees. Elly spread her ears and flapped them. It was not easy, and Elly couldn't soar. "Oh, dear!" said Elly. "I'm exhausted. I will exercise like Elk instead."

Elly watched Elk fold his slender legs under his body and jump-jump-jump extra fast over the bushes. Elly tried to fold her legs and jump. It was not easy, and Elly couldn't jump. "Oh, dear!" said Elly. "I'm exhausted. I will exercise like Ermine instead."

Elly watched Ermine shimmy-shimmy-shimmy extra fast through the grass. Elly tried to do the same. It was not easy, and Elly couldn't shimmy. "Oh, dear!" sobbed Elly. "I'm exhausted and I still can't exercise like my friends."

"What's the matter, Elly?" asked Eagle, Elk, and Ermine.

"I can't flap-flap-flap, jump-jump-jump, or shimmy-shimmy-shimmy extra fast," said Elly. "I want to exercise the elephant way. That's the exercise that gives me energy!"

Suddenly, Elly's friends understood! Everyone needs to exercise her own way. So they encouraged Elly to enjoy the best exercise for her—a nice slow elephant walk!

 Practice Printing

elephant

E E E E E E E E E E E E E E

E E

E E

e e e e e e e e e e e e e e

e e

e e

Ee Ee Ee Ee Ee Ee Ee Ee Ee

Ee Ee

Ee Ee

Frankie Fish

fish

Read-Aloud Puppet Story

Setting the Stage: Ask children to recall things they may have feared when they were younger. Did any of them feel a fear of moving to a new home or school? Invite volunteers to share their experiences. Then tell students that they will hear a story about a fish who is afraid of many things, including moving to a new home.

Pocket-Chart Poem

Building Reading Skills: Print each line of the poem on a sentence strip. Place strips into a pocket chart. After reciting the poem several times, ask children what other words could substitute for moving day (*swimming away, big fish, anything new,* and so on). Print these variations on separate sentence-strip segments cut to fit over the original words. Have children take turns inserting the word cards into the pocket chart and then reading aloud the new versions.

Extension Activities

Stick Puppet Drama: Invite children to use their stick puppets to act out Frankie Fish's feelings and actions as they occur in the story. Afterward, have children demonstrate the different ways they moved their puppets to show Frankie feeling afraid, Frankie flying in circles, and Frankie flitting up and down, jumping, feasting, and sleeping.

Read the story again so children have a chance to try out the different movements demonstrated.

Important Characters: Have children listen for the different characters as you reread the story. Ask them to name all of the characters mentioned. List their responses on chart paper. Then explain that the main characters appear in most of the story. Often the story is about these characters. The other characters—minor characters—may only be in a small part of the story, but are important because they help tell the story. Afterward, ask children to put a check next to the main characters on the list.

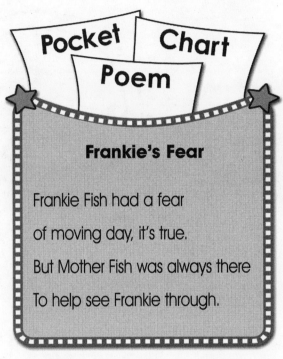

Pocket Chart Poem

Frankie's Fear

Frankie Fish had a fear

of moving day, it's true.

But Mother Fish was always there

To help see Frankie through.

Puppet Pointers

1. Trace the fish onto orange, green, or yellow craft foam. Cut it out.

2. Add details with a fine-tip permanent marker.

3. Glue on wiggle eyes.

4. If desired, use glitter glue to outline fish markings and bubbles.

Stick Puppet Pattern

Directions: Color and cut out the puppet pattern.
Glue a craft-stick handle to the back. Use the puppet
as a storytelling prop.

fish

Ff is for Frankie Fish

Learn-the-Alphabet Puppet Pals Scholastic Professional Books

 # Frankie Fish

fish

Frankie Fish feared almost everything. He was afraid to swim away from Mother Fish to play with his friends. He was afraid of the big fish that swam by on their way to school. And he was afraid of anything new and different.

So when Frankie learned from Mother Fish that they were moving, he felt really afraid! Mother Fish called the move migrating, but Frankie called it frightful.

Frankie knew all about moving. His friends had told him it was frightening. They said that he would have to swim through forceful tides and fight for food. They said moving was no fun.

"I'm afraid," said Frankie on the day of the move.

"Everything will be fine," answered Mother Fish. "Just stay close to my fins."

Together the fish began their migration. They passed a farm. Frankie saw some fowl flying in circles over the water. Frankie pretended to fly in circles near his mother's fins. What fun!

They passed four fish flitting up and down. Frankie flitted up and down near his mother's fins. What fun!

They passed five frogs jumping in the foam. Frankie jumped in the foam near his mother's fins. What fun!

Soon, Mother Fish announced, "We're here!" Frankie looked up and saw a field of ferns ahead. Food!

After his feast of fern, Frankie said, "Moving isn't frightful." His sleepy head fell against Mother Fish's fin. "Moving is fun. My only fear now is that we might never move again." And he then fell fast asleep.

Practice Printing

fish

Name

F F F F F F F F F F F F

F F

F F

f f f f f f f f f f f f

f f

f f

Ff Ff Ff Ff Ff Ff Ff Ff

Ff Ff

Ff Ff

Greta Goat

goat

Read-Aloud Puppet Story

Setting the Stage: Ask children to discuss their feelings about playing in dirt and mud. What do grown-ups think about kids having fun this way? After sharing, tell students that they will hear a story about a goat who loves to play in the garden.

Pocket-Chart Poem

Building Reading Skills: Print each line of the poem on a sentence strip. Place strips into a pocket chart. After reciting the poem several times, ask children what other words could substitute for garden grime (*garden greens, garden goop, garden grit,* and so on). Print these variations on separate sentence-strip segments cut to fit over the original words. Have children take turns inserting the word cards into the pocket chart and then reading aloud the new versions.

Extension Activities

Stick Puppet Drama: Invite children to use their stick puppets to act out Greta Goat's feelings and actions as they occur in the story. Afterward, have children demonstrate the different ways they moved their puppets to show Greta getting dirty, Greta getting groomed and glamorous, and Greta "grinning" because Kitty loved her no matter what she looked like.

Read the story again so children have a chance to try out the different movements demonstrated.

Listen for G: Tell children that Greta Goat's name begins with the sound for *g*. To help them identify this sound in the story, ask children to place their puppets in their laps. Explain that, as you read the story, they should lift their Greta puppet each time they hear a word that begins with *g*. When children perform this action, pause and write the identified word on your alphabet word wall or chart paper. At the end of the story, review all the *g* words with students.

Pocket Chart Poem

Greta Gets Glamorous

Greta Goat loved the garden grime.

Her coat was always a mess.

But a visit to a glamour party

helped Greta look her best.

Puppet Pointers

1. Glue craft fur or terry cloth to the goat shape. Trim the excess material.

2. Add details with fine-tip permanent marker.

3. Add wiggle eyes and yarn whiskers.

4. For story props, make a few "glamorous" ribbon bows and fray the ends of some "grimy" brown felt pieces. Back these with tape loops or self-adhesive dots, so you can place them and remove them to tell the story.

Stick Puppet Pattern

Directions: Color and cut out the puppet pattern.
Glue a craft-stick handle to the back. Use the puppet
as a storytelling prop.

goat

Gg is for Greta Goat

Greta Goat

goat

Greta Goat loved to slip through the garden gate to play. After a day in the garden, Greta's coat was covered with garden grime, garden greens, garden goop, and garden grit.

One day, Greta received an invitation to Kitty's party.

On the day of the party, Greta left the garden to go to Kitty's house. As usual, she was covered with garden grime, garden greens, garden goop, and garden grit. When she arrived, Greta found the guests being groomed and made to look glamorous.

When it was time for Greta's glamour grooming, the host cleaned and brushed Greta's coat. She tied pretty bows in Greta's hair and sprayed geranium perfume behind her ears. Greta glanced into a mirror. Goodness! How glamorous she looked! Greta grinned from ear to ear. At that moment, Kitty snapped a photo of Greta with her camera. "You look great!" Kitty told her.

But Greta did not stay glamorous for long. On the way home, she stopped at the garden. Soon, her glamorous looks disappeared under layers of garden grime, garden greens, garden goop, and garden grit.

That night, Greta looked in the mirror. "I'm hopeless," she thought sadly. "No one wants a grubby friend like me." Greta cried herself to sleep.

On her way to the garden the next day, Greta found a photo pinned to the gate. On the back was a note that read: "Whether you're grubby or gorgeous, it's true we'll always be friends through and through." It was a picture of Greta at Kitty's glamour party. And Greta grinned from ear to ear!

 **Practice Printing**

goat

Name

G G G G G G G G G G G

G G

G G

g g g g g g g g g g g

g g

g g

Gg Gg Gg Gg Gg Gg Gg

Gg Gg

Gg Gg

Harry Horse

horse

Read-Aloud Puppet Story

Setting the Stage: Ask children to share their experiences with hiccups. Were they able to make their hiccups go away? Tell students that they will hear a story about a horse who can't get rid of his hiccups.

Pocket-Chart Poem

Building Reading Skills: Print each line of the poem on a sentence strip. Place strips into a pocket chart. After reciting the poem several times, ask children what other words could substitute for nibbled hay (*sipped on honey, stood on his head,* and so on). Print these variations on separate sentence-strip segments cut to fit over the original words. Have children take turns inserting the word cards into the pocket chart and then reading aloud the new versions.

Extension Activities

Stick Puppet Drama: Invite children to use their stick puppets to act out Harry Horse's feelings and actions as they occur in the story. Afterward, have children demonstrate the different ways they moved their puppets to show Harry having hiccups, Harry nibbling hay and sipping honey, Harry standing on his head, and Harry slamming down his hoof, hopping, and dancing.

Read the story again so children have a chance to try out the different movements demonstrated.

A Solution to the Problem: Have children describe in their own words the solution to Harry's problem. Then invite them to write about and illustrate hiccup cures that they may have tried. Bind student pages into a class book titled *How to Cure the Hiccups.* Add the book to your class library.

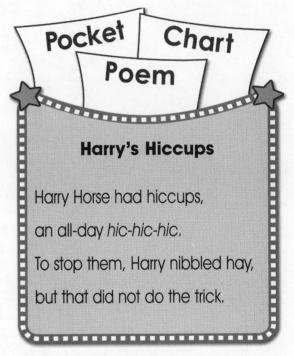

Pocket Chart Poem

Harry's Hiccups

Harry Horse had hiccups,

an all-day *hic-hic-hic.*

To stop them, Harry nibbled hay,

but that did not do the trick.

Puppet Pointers

1. Glue craft fur or terry cloth to the horse shape. Trim the excess material.

2. Add details with a fine-tip permanent marker.

3. Glue on wiggle eyes.

4. Add a yarn mane and a fabric blanket.

Stick Puppet Pattern

Directions: Color and cut out the puppet pattern.
Glue a craft-stick handle to the back. Use the puppet
as a storytelling prop.

horse

Hh is for Harry Horse

Learn-the-Alphabet Puppet Pals Scholastic Professional Books

Harry Horse

horse

Harry Horse had the hiccups. At first, having the hiccups was fun. *Hic-hic-hic!* The other horses at Horse Ring Riding School laughed and laughed. They thought Harry's hiccups were hysterical. But when Harry's hiccups lasted for hours, Hannah Horse began to worry.

"Try nibbling on some hay," said Hannah. So Harry nibbled on some hay. *Hic-hic-hic!* His hiccups did not go away.

"Try sipping some honey," said Hannah. So Harry sipped some honey. *Hic-hic-hic!* His hiccups did not go away.

"Stand on your head!" said Hannah. So Harry stood on his head (a hard thing for a horse, indeed). *Hic-hic-hic!* His hiccups did not go away.

"It's no use!" whinnied Hannah. "The hay and the honey did not make your hiccups go away. Standing on your head didn't work either. You're going to be hiccupping *forever!*"

On hearing that, Harry lifted his front hoof and stamped it down hard. It landed squarely on top of his other hoof. *Ouch-ouch-ouch!* The pain caused Harry to hold his breath while he hopped round and round rubbing his hurt hoof. When he finally gasped for air, Harry's hoof pain was gone. And so were his hiccups!

"Hip-hip-hooray!" said Harry as he happily danced around Hannah. "No more hiccups!"

Practice Printing

horse

Name

Iggy Iguana

Read-Aloud Puppet Story

Setting the Stage: Invite children to tell about ways in which they might be considered picky eaters. Ask them to explain why they choose not to eat certain foods. After sharing, tell students that they will hear a story about an iguana who refuses to eat.

Pocket-Chart Poem

Building Reading Skills: Print each line of the poem on a sentence strip. Place strips into a pocket chart. After reciting the poem several times, ask children what other words could substitute for insect mix (*fruit bits*, *cold milk*, and so on). Print these variations on separate sentence-strip segments cut to fit over the original words. Have children take turns inserting the word cards into the pocket chart and then reading aloud the new versions.

Extension Activities

Stick Puppet Drama: Invite children to use their stick puppets to act out Iggy Iguana's feelings and actions as they occur in the story. Afterward, have children demonstrate the different ways they moved their puppets to show Iggy refusing food, Iggy laughing and catching food on his tongue, and Iggy willing to taste new foods.

Read the story again so children have a chance to try out the different movements demonstrated.

Foods with Short I: Give children paper and crayons. Then reread the story. Ask children to draw and label each food named. Afterward, have them circle the foods that have the short sound of *i*. On another page, have students draw up to five foods that they personally think are icky. Ask them to share their drawings with the class. Do any of their icky foods have the short sound of *i*? Use this opportunity to help children discover that not everyone considers the same foods to be icky (or yummy).

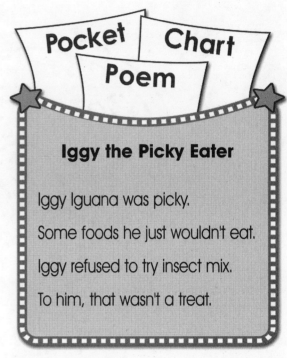

Iggy the Picky Eater

Iggy Iguana was picky,

Some foods he just wouldn't eat.

Iggy refused to try insect mix.

To him, that wasn't a treat.

Puppet Pointers

1. Trace the iguana shape onto green craft foam. Cut it out.

2. Add details with a fine-tip permanent marker.

3. Glue on wiggle eyes.

4. Outline the iguana with green puff paints.

5. Add green glitter glue spots.

Stick Puppet Pattern

Directions: Color and cut out the puppet pattern.
Glue a craft-stick handle to the back. Use the puppet
as a storytelling prop.

iguana

Ii is for Iggy Iguana

x

x

x

Iggy Iguana

Iggy Iguana was a picky eater. He turned his nose up at the insect mix, fruit bits on a stick, and the cold glass of milk that Dad fixed for him.

Dad tried to interest Iggy in the food. "Come on, Iggy," he said. "This mix is filled with fresh, crispy insects! Take a little bite for me."

But Iggy folded his front legs across his thorax, wrinkled his nose, and said, "Insects are icky!"

"Well," Dad pleaded, "have some fruit bits instead."

But Iggy tightened his front legs across his thorax, wrinkled his nose, and said "Fruit bits are sticky!"

"Please eat *something*!" begged Dad. "Here, sip some milk."

But Iggy folded his front legs even tighter across his thorax, wrinkled his nose, and said, "Milk makes me sicky!"

"Oh, Iggy! I don't know what to do with you!" sighed Dad as he picked up the tray of food. "All this iguana food will go to waste."

Just then Dad tripped over a stick. The tray flew into the air and food fell everywhere. Iggy opened his mouth wide and laughed. His long iguana tongue rolled out and was quickly covered with the falling insect mix, fruit bits, and milk.

Iggy jerked his tongue back into his mouth and sat very still. Then he licked his lips. "This food isn't icky. It isn't sticky. And I'm not sicky!" exclaimed Iggy.

From then on, Iggy tasted any kind of food that Dad fixed for him.

Practice Printing

iguana

Name

I I I I I I I I I I I

I   I

I   I

i i i i i i i i i i

i   i

i   i

Ii Ii Ii Ii Ii Ii Ii Ii   Ii

Ii   Ii

Ii   Ii

Jazzy Jaguar

Read-Aloud Puppet Story

Setting the Stage: Have children brainstorm a list of items that people might enjoy collecting. Do students collect any items on the list? After sharing, tell students that they will hear a story about a jaguar who collects jewelry.

Pocket-Chart Poem

Building Reading Skills: Print each line of the poem on a sentence strip. Place strips into a pocket chart. After reciting the poem several times, ask children what other words could substitute for count (*clean, sort, polish, try on, admire,* and so on). Print these variations on separate sentence-strip segments cut to fit over the original words. Have children take turns inserting the word cards into the pocket chart and then reading aloud the new versions.

Extension Activities

Stick Puppet Drama: Invite children to use their stick puppets to act out Jazzy Jaguar's feelings and actions as they occur in the story. Afterward, have children demonstrate the different ways they moved their puppets to show Jazzy counting, cleaning, sorting, and polishing his jewelry. (Tip: Children may want to draw or tape on a paper jewelry box for Jazzy to hold.)

Read the story again so children have a chance to try out the different movements demonstrated.

The Days of the Week: Have children hold their puppets in their laps. Instruct them to listen for the days of the week as you reread the story. Each time students hear the name of a day, have them raise their puppets. Write each identified day on a separate sentence strip. Afterward, invite children to place the sentence strips in your pocket chart to show the correct sequence for the days of the week.

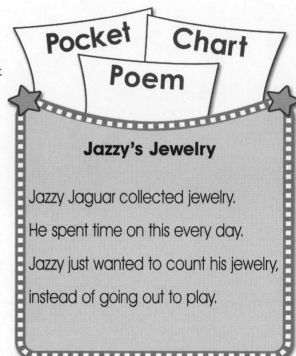

Jazzy's Jewelry

Jazzy Jaguar collected jewelry.

He spent time on this every day.

Jazzy just wanted to count his jewelry,

instead of going out to play.

Puppet Pointers

1. Glue craft fur or terry cloth to the jaguar. Trim the excess material.

2. Add details with a fine-tip permanent marker.

3. Glue on wiggle eyes.

4. Use glitter glue to decorate the jewelry. Or use toy jewelry as a story prop.

5. Cut out a jewelry box from brown craft foam. Tape to puppet to tell the story.

Stick Puppet Pattern

Directions: Color and cut out the puppet pattern.
Glue a craft-stick handle to the back. Use the puppet
as a storytelling prop.

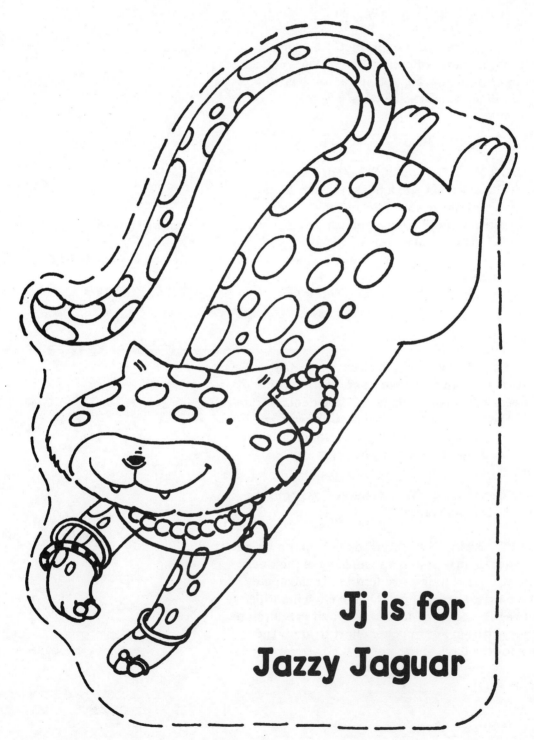

Jj is for
Jazzy Jaguar

Jazzy Jaguar

Jazzy Jaguar loved jewelry. He liked jangly bracelets, jazzy necklaces, and jingly rings. Instead of playing, Jazzy spent his days with his jewelry collection.

One Monday, Blue Jay asked Jazzy to play. "I can't play today," said Jazzy. "I have to count my jewelry."

On Tuesday, Blue Jay asked Jazzy to play. "I can't today," said Jazzy. "I have to clean my jewelry."

On Wednesday, Blue Jay asked again. "Not today," said Jazzy. "I have to sort my jewelry."

On Thursday, Jazzy said, "Today, I have to polish my jewelry."

On Friday, Jazzy had to try on his jewelry. And on Saturday, he had to admire his jewelry. By this time, Blue Jay felt quite jealous of Jazzy's jewelry.

So early Sunday morning, Blue Jay flew to Jazzy's home. While Jazzy slept, Blue Jay hid his jewelry box in a nearby tree. When Jazzy woke up, Blue Jay asked, "Do you want to play *today*?"

"Yes, Blue Jay!" exclaimed Jazzy. "Today, I do want to play. Just let me put on my jewelry first." Jazzy looked around, but he did not see his jewelry box. It was gone! Jazzy began to cry.

Surprised at his friend's tears, Blue Jay told Jazzy the truth. "I hid your jewelry because I was jealous. I miss playing with my friend." Then Blue Jay brought the jewelry box back to Jazzy.

Jazzy joyfully accepted the box. He placed a jazzy necklace around Blue Jay's neck. Then he promised to play with his friend every day.

Practice Printing

jaguar

Name

J J J J J J J J J J J J J J J J J

J J

J J

j j j j j j j j j j j j j j j

j j

j j

J j J j J j J j J j J j J j J j

J j J j

J j J j

Kerry Koala

koala

Read-Aloud Puppet Story

Setting the Stage: Invite children to tell about times when they felt nervous or afraid to leave their mothers or fathers. Did they do anything special to ease their fears? After discussing, tell students that they will hear a story about a little koala who is afraid to leave her mother.

Pocket-Chart Poem

Building Reading Skills: Print each line of the poem on a sentence strip. Place strips into a pocket chart. After reciting the poem several times, ask children what other words could substitute for circle time *(story time, snack time, rest time,* and so on). Print these variations on separate sentence-strip segments cut to fit over the original words. Have children take turns inserting the word cards into the pocket chart and then reading aloud the new versions.

Extension Activities

Stick Puppet Drama: Invite children to use their stick puppets to act out Kerry Koala's feelings and actions as they occur in the story. Afterward, have children demonstrate the different ways they moved their puppets to show Kerry walking to school, Kerry feeling sad and sobbing, Kerry squeezing the keychain during circle time, story time, snack time, and rest time, and Kerry running into her house and being excited that her day went so well. (Tip: Children may want to draw or tape a paper keychain to Kerry.)

Read the story again so children have a chance to try out the different movements demonstrated.

Learn About Setting: Ask children to identify the three settings as you reread the story (Kerry's home, the path to school, and the classroom). Then divide the class into three groups. Have each group decorate a sheet of bulletin-board paper with a scene to represent one of the story settings. Display the completed scenes on a wall. Invite children to use their puppets and the background scenes to retell the story.

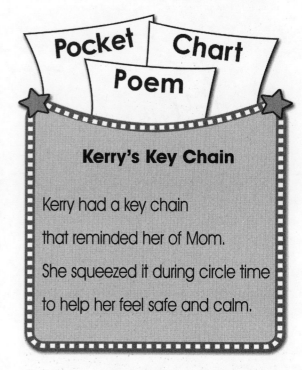

Pocket Chart Poem

Kerry's Key Chain

Kerry had a key chain

that reminded her of Mom.

She squeezed it during circle time

to help her feel safe and calm.

Puppet Pointers

1. Glue craft fur or terry cloth to the koala shape. Trim the excess material.

2. Add wiggle eyes and black felt or button noses.

3. Use a real key chain as a story prop.

Stick Puppet Pattern

Directions: Color and cut out the puppet pattern.
Glue a craft-stick handle to the back. Use the puppet
as a storytelling prop.

koala

Kk is for

Kerry Koala

Kerry Koala

"Today is the first day of kindergarten!" said Mother Koala.

Kerry smiled. She wanted to look brave. But secretly, she did not want to leave Mother.

When Kerry was ready to go, Father took a picture of Kerry and Mother together. Then Mother took the picture into the kitchen to make a secret keepsake for Kerry.

As they walked along the path to school, Kerry squeezed Mother's paw tightly. When Kerry was able to see the school, she began to sob, "I don't want to go to kindergarten. I want to stay with you, Mother!"

Mother hugged Kerry. "You'll like school. I have just the thing to help you enjoy the day." Mother reached into her pouch and pulled out a heart-shaped key chain. She opened the heart and held it out to Kerry. Inside the little heart frame was the picture of Kerry and Mother!

"This is a keepsake key chain," said Mother. "Whenever you miss me, just squeeze the heart and you will feel my love." Then Mother slipped the key chain into Kerry's paw.

Throughout the day, Kerry knew just what to do when she missed Mother. She squeezed the keepsake key chain during circle time, story time, snack time, and rest time.

"Kindergarten was great!" said Kerry as she ran into the kitchen to Mother.

"I'm glad!" said Mother. "Tell me what you like most about kindergarten."

"Well, I like circle time, story time, snack time, and even rest time," Kerry answered. "But best of all, I like keepsake key chain time!"

Practice Printing

koala

Name

K K K K K K K K K K K K K K K

K K

K K

k k k k k k k k k k k k

k k

k k

Kk Kk Kk Kk Kk Kk Kk Kk Kk

Kk Kk

Kk Kk

Lolly Lamb

lamb

Read-Aloud Puppet Story

Setting the Stage: Ask children to tell about times when they did not want to share their belongings. Did this affect their friendships? After sharing, tell children that they will hear a story about a lamb whose unwillingness to share got her into a big mess.

Pocket-Chart Poem

Building Reading Skills: Print each line of the poem on a sentence strip. Place strips into a pocket chart. After reciting the poem several times, ask children what other words could substitute for lemon (*lime, licorice,* and so on). Print these variations on separate sentence-strip segments cut to fit over the original words. Have children take turns inserting the word cards into the pocket chart and then reading aloud the new versions.

Extension Activities

Stick Puppet Drama: Invite children to use their stick puppets to act out Lolly Lamb's feelings and actions as they occur in the story. Afterward, have children demonstrate the different ways they moved their puppets to show Lolly licking, Lolly sleeping, Lolly waking up, and Lolly happy to be clean again. (Tip: Have children tape removable paper lollipops to Lolly's coat. Also, offer children real or paper lollipops for Lolly to lick.)

Read the story again so children have a chance to try out the different movements demonstrated.

Listen for L: Explain to children that Lolly Lamb's name begins with the sound for *l.* Say her name several times to reinforce the sound. Then ask students to hold their puppets in their laps as you reread the story. When they hear Lolly's name—or any other word beginning with *l*—have children loop their puppets over their heads and back into their laps. To extend, ask children to brainstorm a list of *l* words to describe lollipops (these might be flavor, shape, size, or color words). Write the words on a large paper lollipop to display on your alphabet word wall.

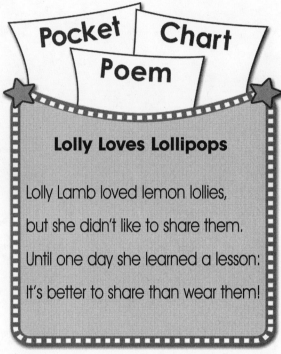

Pocket Chart Poem

Lolly Loves Lollipops

Lolly Lamb loved lemon lollies,

but she didn't like to share them.

Until one day she learned a lesson:

It's better to share than wear them!

Puppet Pointers

1. Glue the pattern onto oaktag. Cut it out.

2. Glue craft fur, felt, or terry cloth to the lamb shape. Trim the excess material.

3. Add wiggle eyes and felt ears.

4. Glue a craft-stick handle to the back.

Stick Puppet Pattern

Directions: Color and cut out the puppet pattern.
Glue a craft-stick handle to the back. Use the puppet
as a storytelling prop.

lamb

Ll is for Lolly Lamb

Lolly Lamb

lamb

Lolly Lamb loved lollipops. Her favorites were lemon, lime, and licorice lollies. But she also loved lollipops in all flavors, sizes, shapes, and colors.

Lolly didn't share her lollipops with her little lamb friends. Instead, she unwrapped and licked each lollipop with the other lambs looking on. After a few licks, Lolly would lay her lollipop down and leave. She left lollies almost anywhere—the living room, the library, and even the laundry room.

One day, Lolly sat in the living room licking lollipops while the other lambs played outside. She licked and licked, trying to decide which lollipop she liked best. But she couldn't decide, and all that licking made her tired. Lolly laid her head back and fell asleep.

Lolly awoke later to find lollipops stuck all over her coat. She pulled at the lollipops, but they stuck tight. Lolly began to cry.

Luckily, her lamb friends heard her. "What's wrong, Lolly?" they called out. Looking out the window, Lolly told the lambs about her problem.

"We can help!" they said. "Come out here. We know what to do."

Lolly stepped outside. The other lambs began to lick the lollipops on her coat. They licked and licked. Soon, all the candy was gone and the sticks fell to the ground. Lolly looked at her clean coat and exclaimed, "Lollipops for everyone! Come on!"

The lambs laughed and followed Lolly inside. From then on, Lolly shared all her lollipops with her friends. And, from then on, she always licked her own lollipop right down to the stick.

Practice Printing

lamb

Name

Matty Mouse

mouse

Read-Aloud Puppet Story

Setting the Stage: Invite children to share their experiences about times when grown-ups paid more attention to younger children or babies than to them. How did this make them feel? After discussing, tell children that they will hear a story about a little mouse who gets a lot of attention from grown-ups.

Pocket-Chart Poem

Building Reading Skills: Print each line of the poem on a sentence strip. Place strips into a pocket chart. After reciting the poem several times, ask children what other words could substitute for marching (*playing toss, toasting marshmallows,* and so on). Print these variations on separate sentence-strip segments cut to fit over the original words. Have children take turns inserting the word cards into the pocket chart and then reading aloud the new versions.

Extension Activities

Stick Puppet Drama: Invite children to use their stick puppets to act out Mattie Mouse's feelings and actions as they occur in the story. Afterward, have children demonstrate the different ways they moved their puppets to show Mattie acting sweet, Mattie hiding under the table and tugging tails, Mattie talking to the other mouse children, and Mattie having fun. (Tip: Use the Mattie Mouse pattern to make other mice to represent the mouse children.)

Read the story again so children have a chance to try out the different movements demonstrated.

Problems and Solutions: Explain to students that every story has a major conflict, or problem. Ask them to listen for the major conflict as you reread the story. Then decide as a class what the story's major conflict is (Matty is a mischievous mouse). Write it inside a large circle on chart paper. Then draw lines from the circle. Encourage children to name other problems that stemmed from the story's major conflict (others get blamed for Matty's mischievousness, grown-ups refuse to believe that Matty is mischievous, Matty does not get corrected for misbehaving, etc.). Write each different response on a line. Repeat this exercise with other stories in this book.

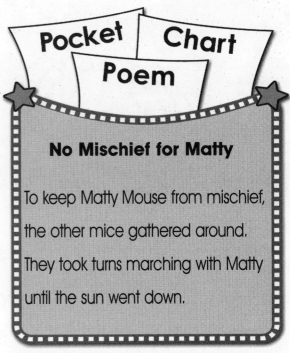

Pocket Chart Poem

No Mischief for Matty

To keep Matty Mouse from mischief,

the other mice gathered around.

They took turns marching with Matty

until the sun went down.

Puppet Pointers

1. Glue craft fur, felt, or terry cloth to the mouse shape. Trim the excess material.

2. Add wiggle eyes and a yarn or ribbon tail.

Stick Puppet Pattern

Directions: Color and cut out the puppet pattern. Glue a craft-stick handle to the back. Use the puppet as a storytelling prop.

mouse

Mm is for Matty Mouse

Learn-the-Alphabet Puppet Pals Scholastic Professional Books

 # Matty Mouse

mouse

When Mother Mouse went out with little Matty, the grown-up mice always *oohed* and *aahed* over him.

"He's perfect!" "He's sweet." "There's not a mischievous bone in his body," the grown-ups said.

The mouse children just rolled their eyes. They knew that Matty did have a mischievous side. In fact, it was Matty who ruined last year's Annual Mouse Picnic. He hid under the tables and tugged their tails. This made the mice spill their milk and make a mess.

But the grown-up mice didn't believe that Matty could do such things. They blamed the older mice and made them mop up the mess.

With this year's picnic just a day away, the mice children agreed that something had to be done about Matty. But what?

"If we leave Matty alone, he'll make mischief," sighed Mindy.

"And we'll be blamed," said Mike.

But Mariah had a plan.

When Matty arrived at the picnic, the mouse children gathered around him. They began to argue over who would march with Matty in the picnic parade. And who would play milk-bottle toss and toast marshmallows with him. "My, my!" shouted Matty. "I'm small, but there's enough of me to go around! You can take turns."

So all day, the mouse children took turns minding Matty. Matty had such fun that he forgot to make mischief.

When Mother picked up Matty at the end of the day, the grown-ups all called him a perfect little mouse. The mouse children just winked at each other and smiled.

Practice Printing

mouse

Name

M M M M M M M M M M M

M M

M M

m m m m m m m m m m m

m m

m m

Mm Mm Mm Mm Mm Mm Mm

Mm Mm

Mm Mm

Dr. Nancy Newt

newt

Read-Aloud Puppet Story

Setting the Stage: Invite children to share about their experiences when visiting a doctor. Did they get a shot? How did they react? After sharing, tell students that they will hear a story about a doctor who doesn't like to give shots to kids.

Pocket-Chart Poem

Building Reading Skills: Print each line of the poem on a sentence strip. Place strips into a pocket chart. After reciting the poem several times, ask children what other words could substitute for *checked their eyes* (*listened to their hearts, looked in their ears, took their temperatures, prescribed their medicine,* and so on). Print these variations on separate sentence-strip segments cut to fit over the original words. Have children take turns inserting the word cards into the pocket chart and then reading aloud the new versions.

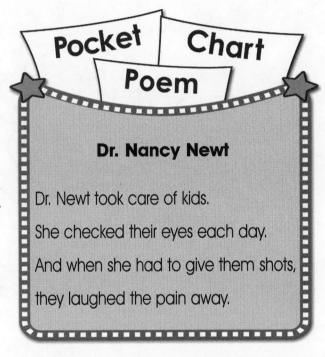

Pocket Chart Poem

Dr. Nancy Newt

Dr. Newt took care of kids.

She checked their eyes each day.

And when she had to give them shots,

they laughed the pain away.

Extension Activities

Stick Puppet Drama: Invite children to use their stick puppets to act out Dr. Nancy Newt's feelings and actions as they occur in the story. Afterward, have children demonstrate the different ways they moved their puppets to show Nancy examining patients, Nancy tossing and turning in bed, Nancy whispering, and Nancy giving out clown stickers.

Read the story again so children have a chance to try out the different movements demonstrated.

Listen for N: Explain to children that Dr. Nancy Newt's name begins with the sound for *n*. Say her name several times to reinforce the sound. Then have children hold their puppets in their laps as you reread the story. When they hear Dr. Newt's name—or any other word beginning with *n*—have children touch their puppets to their noses.

Puppet Pointers

1. Trace the newt onto green craft foam. Cut it out.

2. Add details with a fine-tip permanent marker.

3. Add wiggle eyes. If desired, also add fabric pieces for clothing.

4. Highlight the needle in the pocket with silver glitter glue.

5. Glue the pattern onto oaktag. Cut it out.

6. Glue a craft-stick handle to the back.

Stick Puppet Pattern

Directions: Color and cut out the puppet pattern.
Glue a craft-stick handle to the back. Use the puppet
as a storytelling prop.

newt

Nn is for Nancy Newt

Dr. Nancy Newt

newt

Dr. Nancy Newt loved taking care of children. She checked their eyes, listened to their hearts, looked in their ears, took their temperatures, and prescribed their medicine. And she gave them nifty clown stickers.

The only part of her job that Dr. Newt didn't like was giving shots. She didn't want children to hurt or cry when she used a needle for their medicine.

One night, Dr. Newt tossed and turned in bed. She couldn't sleep. She was trying to think of a new way to make needles hurt less. Over and over she thought, "Nice Nancy Newt's needles need not hurt." After a while, the words ran together and sounded silly. Dr. Newt laughed out loud. Suddenly, she had an idea!

The next day, Nicky and Nina visited Dr. Newt. They both needed a shot. Nicky was first. Dr. Newt whispered into his ear. "I'll try," he said.

Then Nicky pinched his nose and said, "Nicky paid nine nickels for a neat, nifty necklace." He repeated the words until they ran together. Nicky laughed.

"Done!" announced Dr. Newt.

"Wow! I didn't feel any pain," Nicky said with surprise.

"My turn," said Nina as she pinched her nose and began, "Nina paid nine nickels for a neat, nifty necklace." When the words became silly, Nancy started to laugh.

Dr. Newt smiled and put away her needle. She gave each child a nifty clown sticker. And because she was so pleased with her new, no-pain way to give shots, Dr. Newt gave herself a sticker, too.

Practice Printing

newt

Name

N N N N N N N N N N N N

N N

N N

n n n n n n n n n n n n n

n n

n n

Nn Nn Nn Nn Nn Nn Nn Nn

Nn Nn

Nn Nn

Olive Octopus

Read-Aloud Puppet Story

Setting the Stage: Ask children to share their knowledge of operas with the class. Afterward, explain that an opera tells a story in song. Tell students that they will hear a story about an octopus who dreams of being an opera singer.

Pocket-Chart Poem

Building Reading Skills: Print each line of the poem on a sentence strip. Place strips into a pocket chart. After reciting the poem several times, ask children what other words could substitute for opera (*old tunes*, *new tunes*, *bold tunes*, *show tunes*, and so on). Print these variations on separate sentence-strip segments cut to fit over the original words. Have children take turns inserting the word cards into the pocket chart and then reading aloud the new versions.

Extension Activities

Stick Puppet Drama: Invite children to use their stick puppets to act out Olive Octopus's feelings and actions as they occur in the story. Afterward, have children demonstrate the different ways they moved their puppets to show Olive singing and using puppets. (Tip: Have children draw or tape on paper puppets for Olive to hold.)

Read the story again so children have a chance to try out the different movements demonstrated.

Sing a Vowel Opera: Explain to children that Olive Octopus's name begins with the short sound for *o*. Repeat her name to reinforce the sound. Then have children hold their puppets in their laps as you reread the story. Instruct them to use their puppets to draw an *o* in the air each time they hear a word that begins with short *o*. To review the short *o* sound, invite children to sing this song to the tune of "Mary Had a Little Lamb." Ask them to sing the last line in their best opera voices.

> Ŏlive loved to sing ŏpera,
> sing ŏpera, sing ŏpera.
> Ŏlive loved to sing ŏpera,
> Ŏ-ŏ-ŏ-ŏ-ŏ!

Invite children to repeat the song, using a different vowel sound for the last line.

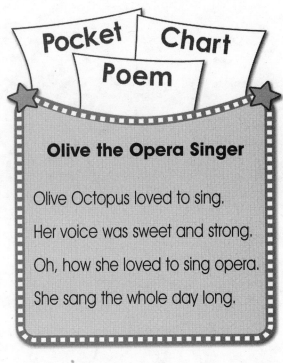

Pocket Chart Poem

Olive the Opera Singer

Olive Octopus loved to sing.

Her voice was sweet and strong.

Oh, how she loved to sing opera.

She sang the whole day long.

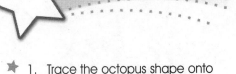

Puppet Pointers

1. Trace the octopus shape onto green or purple craft foam.

2. Add details with a fine-tip permanent marker.

3. Glue on wiggle eyes.

4. Use glitter glue to outline the suction cups on the octopus legs.

5. Cut out puppet characters described in story from foam. Tape to puppet to tell story.

Stick Puppet Pattern

Directions: Color and cut out the puppet pattern.
Glue a craft-stick handle to the back. Use the puppet
as a storytelling prop.

octopus

Oo is for Olive Octopus

Olive Octopus

Olive Octopus liked to sing. She sang old tunes, new tunes, bold tunes, and show tunes. Olive especially liked opera. She loved to sing the different parts of an opera story.

Olive could sing the high, low, and in-between parts of any song. But Mr. Oscar Octopus would not hire Olive to sing at the Underwater Opera House. He said it would be too odd to have an octopus in an opera. Dolphins, whales, and seals sang opera, but no one had ever heard of an opera-singing octopus! Mr. Oscar advised Olive to find a different job.

At first, Olive cried and cried. She didn't want to find a different job. She wanted to sing opera. Finally, she stopped crying. She had to prove that she had talent. And she knew what she needed to do.

The next time Olive's friends saw her, they couldn't believe their eyes. She held an otter puppet in one arm and an osprey puppet in another. She held an ox and octopus puppet in two more arms. Each puppet sang the part of a different opera character. And Olive supplied the voice for every one of them!

When Mr. Oscar heard the news, he swam over to see Olive perform. He was very surprised by her talent.

"Olive, you sing opera beautifully. I want you to sing at the Underwater Opera House tonight!" offered Mr. Oscar.

On hearing this, Olive sang a song of joy with each of her opera puppets.

Practice Printing

Name

Patti Poodle

poodle

Read-Aloud Puppet Story

Setting the Stage: Invite children to share about times when they discovered they did something well. How did they feel at these times? After discussing, tell students that they will hear a story about a poodle who discovers something that she does well.

Pocket-Chart Poem

Building Reading Skills: Print each line of the poem on a sentence strip. Place strips into a pocket chart. After reciting the poem several times, ask children what other words could substitute for lift her paws *(jump over puddles, push open doors, push a carriage, pedal a bicycle, jump through a hoop, balance on a pole, pop through a tunnel, and so on)*. Print these variations on separate sentence-strip segments cut to fit over the original words. Have children take turns inserting the word cards into the pocket chart and then reading aloud the new versions.

Extension Activities

Stick Puppet Drama: Invite children to use their stick puppets to act out Patti Poodle's feelings and actions as they occur in the story. Afterward, have children demonstrate the different ways they moved their puppets to show Patti playing, Patti practicing her lessons, Patti in TV commercials, and Patti performing circus tricks. (Tip: Children may want to draw a tutu on Patti.)

Read the story again so children have a chance to try out the different movements demonstrated.

Patti's Party Picks: Explain that Patti is planning a party and she wants to include items that begin with *p*, the letter at the beginning of her name. Ask children to hold their puppets in their laps. Then tell them that you will call out an item. If the word begins with *p*, they should hold their puppets over their heads. If not, the puppets should remain in their laps. Call out one word at a time, some beginning with *p* and some beginning with other sounds. As children identify the *p* words, write them on a chart to add to your alphabet word wall. (Some *p* words you might include are: pizza, presents, plates, popcorn, punch, puppets, and petunias.)

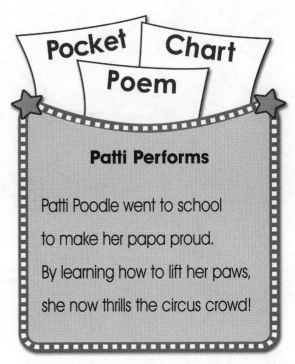

Pocket Chart Poem

Patti Performs

Patti Poodle went to school

to make her papa proud.

By learning how to lift her paws,

she now thrills the circus crowd!

Puppet Pointers

1. Glue craft fur, felt, or cotton balls to the poodle shape. Trim the excess material.

2. Add wiggle eyes and felt ears.

3. Cut a tutu from lace or a piece of tulle. Cut short lengths of ribbon to use for tying on bows and bracelets. Tape these to the puppet to tell the story.

Stick Puppet Pattern

Directions: Color and cut out the puppet pattern. Glue a craft-stick handle to the back. Use the puppet as a storytelling prop.

poodle

Pp is for Patti Poodle

Learn-the-Alphabet Puppet Pals Scholastic Professional Books

Patti Poodle

Patti Poodle loved to play, play, play. But Papa had big ideas for his daughter. He enrolled Patti in school so she could learn to perform tricks. He hoped that she would be in television commercials one day.

Patti did not want to perform tricks for television commercials, but she did want to make Papa proud. So Patti went to school and practiced her lessons every day. Her teacher, Ms. Pouf, taught Patti how to lift her paws, jump over puddles, and push open doors. Patti even learned how to push a doll carriage.

Patti passed school with good grades. She was offered many roles in television commercials selling everything from puppy food to potato puffs. But Patti was not happy being a commercial pup.

One day, Patti took a job for a different kind of commercial. This one advertised a circus.

Patti enjoyed learning tricks for the circus commercial. They were playful and fun. She learned how to pedal a purple bicycle and jump through a hoop onto a pink pillow. She learned how to balance on a tall pole and to pop through a paper tunnel. Plus, Patti got to wear a puffy little tutu!

Ms. Pouf told Papa that she had never seen Patti look so pleased. The circus people agreed. And they liked Patti's performance so much that they offered her a permanent job! When Papa heard the news, he practically popped with pride.

Practice Printing

poodle

Name

P P P P P P P P P P P P

P P

P P

p p p p p p p p p p p p

p p

p p

Pp Pp Pp Pp Pp Pp Pp Pp

Pp Pp

Pp Pp

Quilting Queen

queen

Read-Aloud Puppet Story

Setting the Stage: Invite children to share about times when they've become frustrated or discouraged, learning something new. Then tell students that they will hear a story about a queen who wants to learn how to quilt.

Pocket-Chart Poem

Building Reading Skills: Print each line of the poem on a sentence strip. Place strips into a pocket chart. After reciting the poem several times, ask children what other words could substitute for cut the fabric (*thread the needle, poke the needle, sew fancy stitches,* and so on). Print these variations on separate sentence-strip segments cut to fit over the original words. Have children take turns inserting the word cards into the pocket chart and then reading aloud the new versions.

Extension Activities

Stick Puppet Drama: Invite children to use their stick puppets to act out Quilting Queen's feelings and actions as they occur in the story. Afterward, have children demonstrate the different ways they moved their puppets to show the Queen quivering at the thought of quilting, the Queen becoming upset at her quilting abilities, the Queen sleeping, and the Queen dancing. (Tip: Children may want to make paper quilts for the Queen to quilt.)

Read the story again so children have a chance to try out the different movements demonstrated.

Listen for Q: Explain to children that the words *quilt* and *queen* begin with the sound for *q.* Say the words several times to reinforce the sound. Then have students hold their puppets in their laps as you reread the story. When a *q* word is mentioned, instruct half the students to use their puppets to quietly draw a lowercase *q* in the air. Ask the other children to quietly draw an uppercase *Q* with their puppets. To extend, draw a quilt on bulletin board paper. Write all the *q* words from the story on the quilt. Invite children to brainstorm other words to add to the quilt. Display the quilt on your alphabet word wall.

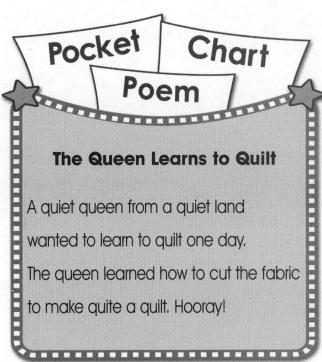

Pocket Chart Poem

The Queen Learns to Quilt

A quiet queen from a quiet land

wanted to learn to quilt one day.

The queen learned how to cut the fabric

to make quite a quilt. Hooray!

Puppet Pointers

1. Cut pieces of fabric into clothing for the queen. Glue the clothes onto the character. Trim the excess material.

2. Add wiggle eyes and yarn hair.

3. Draw additional details with a fine-tip permanent marker.

4. Glue fabric scraps to an old wash-cloth to serve as a quilt.

Stick Puppet Pattern

Directions: Color and cut out the puppet pattern.
Glue a craft-stick handle to the back. Use the puppet
as a storytelling prop.

queen

**Qq is for
Quilting Queen**

Learn-the-Alphabet Puppet Pals Scholastic Professional Books

Quilting Queen

A queen from a quiet land wanted to learn how to quilt. So the royal quilter taught the queen how to cut fabric into squares, how to thread the needle, and how to poke it through the fabric. She even showed the queen some fancy quilt stitches.

Soon, it was the queen's turn to quilt. Her fingers quivered as she set to work. She did everything just as the royal quilter taught her. The queen was sure that she would make quite the perfect quilt.

After quilting all day, the queen finally finished. She stepped back to look at her work. "Oh my!" said the queen, and she began to quake. "The stitches in my quilt are crooked. The squares go this crazy way and that crazy way. My quilt isn't perfect." At that, she dropped onto her throne and sobbed, "I quit!" With the quilt in her lap, the queen cried herself to sleep.

Shortly, the royal quilter stopped by to see the queen. She quietly took the quilt from the sleeping queen's lap and held it up.

"Oh! Look at the queen's quilt!" exclaimed the quilter. "The stitches are so perfectly crooked. And the squares are perfectly sewn in this crazy way and that crazy way. This is quite a quilt!"

The queen heard the royal quilter's words. She jumped up from her throne and began to dance around. She was quite a quilter! She didn't need to quit! From that day on, the queen quilted happily ever after.

Practice Printing

queen

Name

Q Q Q Q Q Q Q Q Q Q

Q   Q

Q   Q

q q q q q q q q q q q q q

q   q

q   q

Qq Qq Qq Qq Qq Qq Qq Qq

Qq   Qq

Qq   Qq

Reluctant Rooster

roaster

Read-Aloud Puppet Story

Setting the Stage: Ask children if they like to stay up past their bedtimes. Is it easy to wake up the next morning after a late night? Tell students that they will hear a story about a rooster who likes to stay up late.

Pocket-Chart Poem

Building Reading Skills: Print each line of the poem on a sentence strip. Place strips into a pocket chart. After reciting the poem several times, ask children what other words could substitute for pig (*horses, cows, sheep, farmer,* and so on). Print these variations on separate sentence-strip segments cut to fit over the original words. Have children take turns inserting the word cards into the pocket chart and then reading aloud the new versions.

Extension Activities

Stick Puppet Drama: Invite children to use their stick puppets to act out Reluctant Rooster's feelings and actions as they occur in the story. Afterward, have children demonstrate the different ways they moved their puppets to show Rooster reciting his rhyme, Rooster feeling worried and staying awake all night, Rooster calling "Cock-a-doodle-do!" and Rooster sleeping.

Read the story again so children have a chance to try out the different movements demonstrated.

Listen for R Words: Explain to children that Rooster's name begins with the sound for *r*. Say his name several times to reinforce the sound. Then have children hold their puppets in their laps. Tell them that you will say three words from the story. If all the words begin with the *r* sound, children should raise their puppets to give a rooster crow. Otherwise, they should keep their puppets in their laps. After naming sets of three words from the story, extend the activity by using words from your alphabet word wall.

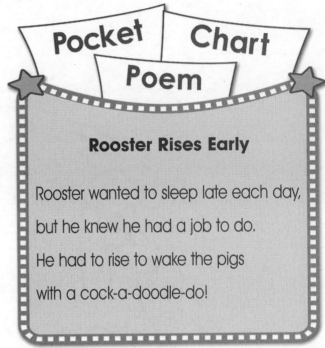

Pocket Chart Poem

Rooster Rises Early

Rooster wanted to sleep late each day,

but he knew he had a job to do.

He had to rise to wake the pigs

with a cock-a-doodle-do!

Puppet Pointers

1. Trace the rooster onto brown craft foam.

2. Add details with a fine-tip permanent marker.

3. Glue on craft feathers and wiggle eyes.

Stick Puppet Pattern

Directions: Color and cut out the puppet pattern.
Glue a craft-stick handle to the back. Use the puppet
as a storytelling prop.

rooster

**Rr is for
Reluctant Rooster**

Learn-the-Alphabet Puppet Pals Scholastic Professional Books

Reluctant Rooster

rooster

Rooster was reluctant to rise early. He knew that a rooster was responsible for waking the pigs horses, cows, sheep, and farmer with his cock-a-doodle-do. But Rooster was not an early bird. He didn't go to bed early, and he didn't get out of bed early.

Rooster's friend, Red Hen, told him her bedtime rule,

"Early to bed
and early to rise
makes a bird healthy,
wealthy, and wise."

But Rooster lived by a different rule:

"Late to bed
and late to rise
makes a bird lazy
and sleepy-eyed."

One day, Rooster heard the farmer talk about a rooster roast. Rooster was really worried. He turned to Red Hen for help. "I have to get to sleep early so I can rise before dawn," he told her.

Red Hen had a plan. She knew Rooster would not be able to wake up in the morning. So that night, Red Hen kept Rooster awake all night long. By dawn, Rooster was still awake. He perched on the fence and cleared his voice. "Cock-a-doodle-do!" The animals and farmer woke up when they heard Rooster's crow.

But Rooster was so tired that he went right to bed. He slept all day and through the night. The next morning, Rooster was up before dawn again. "Cock-a-doodle-do!" His crow woke up the farm. And that became Rooster's routine for the rest of his days.

Practice Printing

rooster

Name

R R R R R R R R R R R

R R

R R

r r r r r r r r r r r r

r r

r

Rr Rr Rr Rr Rr Rr Rr Rr

Rr Rr

Rr Rr

Snake Sisters

snakes

Read-Aloud Puppet Story

Setting the Stage: Invite children to describe ways in which meeting a new friend might have created problems between them and their old friends. After sharing, tell students that they will hear a story about twin snake sisters who meet new friends.

Pocket-Chart Poem

Building Reading Skills: Print each line of the poem on a sentence strip. Place strips into a pocket chart. After reciting the poem several times, ask children what other words could substitute for skiing (*snowboarding, scuba diving, skateboarding, swimming,* and so on). Print these variations on separate sentence-strip segments cut to fit over the original words. Have children take turns inserting the word cards into the pocket chart and then reading aloud the new versions.

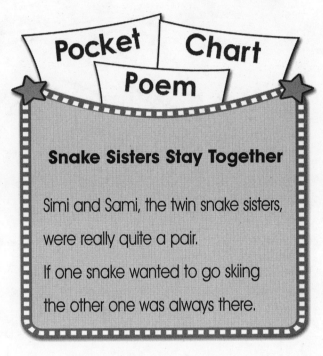

Pocket Chart Poem

Snake Sisters Stay Together

Simi and Sami, the twin snake sisters,

were really quite a pair.

If one snake wanted to go skiing

the other one was always there.

Extension Activities

Stick Puppet Drama: To act out this story, each child will need to make two sets of puppets: One set to represent snake sisters Simi and Sami, the other to represent snake sisters Sorelle and Serena.

Invite children to use their stick puppets to act out the Snake Sisters' feelings and actions as they occur in the story. Afterward, have children demonstrate the different ways they moved their puppets to show the twins skiing, snowboarding, scuba diving, skateboarding, swimming, and sleeping, and all the snakes talking and swinging.

Read the story again so children have a chance to try out the different movements demonstrated.

Listen for S: Explain to children that the words *sisters* and *snakes* begin with the sound for s. Say these words several times to reinforce the sound. Then have children hold their puppets in their laps as you reread the story. When they hear a word beginning with s, have children *hisssss* while drawing an s in the air with their puppets.

Puppet Pointers

⋆ 1. Trace the snake sisters pattern onto green craft foam.

⋆ 2. Add details with a fine-tip permanent marker.

⋆ 3. Glue wiggle eyes on each snake.

⋆ 4. Use glitter glue to outline snake markings.

Stick Puppet Pattern

Directions: Color and cut out the puppet pattern.
Glue a craft-stick handle to the back. Use the puppet
as a storytelling prop.

snakes

Ss is for Snake Sisters

Snake Sisters

snakes

Simi and Sami were twin snake sisters. They were also best friends. The two loved to go skiing, snowboarding, scuba diving, skateboarding, and swimming. Wherever one twin went, the other would also go. And sometimes, the twins didn't go anywhere. They simply curled up and slept side by side.

But the twins were split up at school. Simi went to one class, and Sami went to another.

One day, a new snake named Sorelle came to Simi's class. The teacher asked Simi to be Sorelle's special buddy.

Soon, Simi and Sorelle learned that they had a lot in common. They both loved to swing and seesaw. They loved to sing the same songs. And, they both enjoyed the same storybooks.

"Let's play together after school," suggested Sorelle. "You can come to my new house on Scale Lane."

"Super!" said Simi. She was happy about her new friend, but Simi worried about how to tell Sami.

Simi found Sami after school. Sami was smiling with excitement. "Today, I met a new friend named Serena!" exclaimed Sami. "I'm going to her house on Scale Lane to play."

"Snakes alive!" said Simi. "We both made new friends today."

When the sisters got to Scale Lane, they were surprised to find that their friends lived in the same house. They were even more surprised to learn that their friends were twins, just like them! The four snakes smiled over the situation. Then they all went outside to swing.

Practice Printing

snakes

Name

S S S S S S S S S S S S

S S

S S

s s s s s s s s s s s s s

s s

s s

Ss Ss Ss Ss Ss Ss Ss Ss Ss Ss

Ss Ss

Ss Ss

Timmy Turtle

Read-Aloud Puppet Story

Setting the Stage: Invite children to tell about times when they have been teased. How did it make them feel? What did they do to stop the teasing? After sharing, tell students that they will hear a story about a turtle who gets teased.

Pocket-Chart Poem

Building Reading Skills: Print each line of the poem on a sentence strip. Place strips into a pocket chart. After reciting the poem several times, ask children what other words could substitute for *talked to him* (*teased him back, tattled on him,* and so on). Print these variations on separate sentence-strip segments cut to fit over the original words. Have children take turns inserting the word cards into the pocket chart and then reading aloud the new versions.

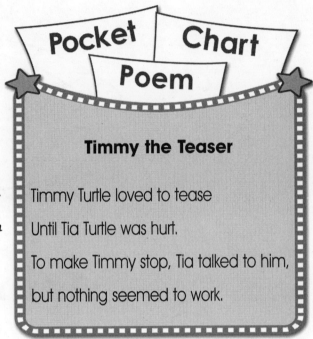

Pocket Chart Poem

Timmy the Teaser

Timmy Turtle loved to tease

Until Tia Turtle was hurt.

To make Timmy stop, Tia talked to him,

but nothing seemed to work.

Extension Activities

Stick Puppet Drama: Invite children to use their stick puppets to act out Timmy and Tia Turtle's feelings and actions as they occur in the story. Afterward, have children demonstrate the different ways they moved their puppets to show Timmy teasing and Tia talking, teasing, tattling, and hiding, and finally, both puppets laughing. (Tip: Have children each use the Timmy Turtle pattern to make a Tia Turtle puppet.)

Read the story again so children have a chance to try out the different movements demonstrated.

Listen for T: Explain to children that Timmy Turtle's name begins with the sound for *t*. Say his name several times to reinforce the sound. Then have children hold their puppets in their laps as you reread the story. When they hear words that begin with the sound of *t*, have children draw a *t* in the air with their puppets. As children identify each *t* word, write it on chart paper. Then invite children to brainstorm other words to add to the list. Display the list on your alphabet word wall.

Puppet Pointers

1. Trace the turtle onto green craft foam.

2. Add details with a fine-tip permanent marker.

3. Use puffy fabric paint to color the cap.

4. Glue on wiggle eyes.

Stick Puppet Pattern

Directions: Color and cut out the puppet pattern.
Glue a craft-stick handle to the back. Use the puppet
as a storytelling prop.

turtle

Tt is for

Timmy Turtle

Learn-the-Alphabet Puppet Pals Scholastic Professional Books

Timmy Turtle

turtle

Timmy Turtle wanted a friend. Tia lived next door to Timmy. She wanted a friend, too.

Tia thought about making Timmy her friend. But Timmy was the type who loved to tease. If Tia lost a game, Timmy teased, "Tia is a loser." If Tia came in second in a race, Timmy teased, "Tia is a slowpoke." And if Tia chose an easy picture book to read, Timmy teased, "Tia is a baby."

Tia tried talking to Timmy about his teasing, but it didn't help. She tried teasing Timmy back, but he just kept on teasing. She even tried tattling, but Timmy's mother didn't know how to stop him either. So Timmy kept on teasing.

Tired of being teased, Tia thought of a plan. The next time Timmy started to tease, Tia said, "Timmy, tell me when you are done teasing forever. That's when I'll be your friend."

Then Tia pulled her head and legs into her shell and ignored Timmy. Oh, how Timmy teased her! "Nya-nya-nya-nya-nya," called Timmy over and over. But Tia sat tight. Timmy teased harder, "Nya-nya-nya-nya-nya." But Tia still sat tight. He teased even harder, "Nya-nya-nya-nya-nya!" Tia didn't budge.

Finally, Timmy got tired of being ignored. "I'm sorry I teased you," he whispered into Tia's shell. "I'll never do it again."

Instantly, Tia popped her head and legs out of her shell. "Terrific!" She smiled. "Now-now-now-now-now we can be friends!"

Tickled by Tia's funny words, the two turtle friends laughed all the way to the playground.

Practice Printing

turtle

Name

Uncle Utz

uncle

Read-Aloud Puppet Story

Setting the Stage: Ask children to share about times when they felt clumsy. How did they overcome their clumsiness? After discussing, tell students that they will hear a story about a very clumsy man and what he does to help get over his clumsiness.

Pocket-Chart Poem

Building Reading Skills: Print each line of the poem on a sentence strip. Place strips into a pocket chart. After reciting the poem several times, ask children what other words could substitute for up, up, up (*over and under, balance on one foot,* and so on). Print these variations on separate sentence-strip segments cut to fit over the original words. Have children take turns inserting the word cards into the pocket chart and then reading aloud the new versions.

Extension Activities

Stick Puppet Drama: Invite children to use their stick puppets to act out Uncle Utz's feelings and actions as they occur in the story. Afterward, have children demonstrate the different ways they moved their puppets to show Uncle Utz bumping into things, Uncle Utz tripping, Uncle Utz practicing dance steps, and Uncle Utz dancing gracefully like a butterfly.

Read the story again so children have a chance to try out the different movements demonstrated.

Listen for U: Explain to children that Uncle Utz's name begins with the short sound for *u*. Say his name several times to reinforce the sound. Then have children hold their puppets in their laps as you reread the story. When they hear Uncle Utz's name—or any other word beginning with the short *u* sound—have children use their puppets to draw a *u* in the air. Record each identified short *u* word on a chart or on your alphabet word wall. To extend, challenge children to add other *u* words to the list.

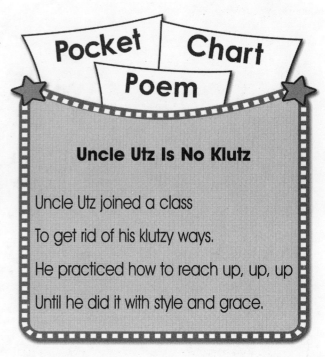

Pocket Chart Poem

Uncle Utz Is No Klutz

Uncle Utz joined a class

To get rid of his klutzy ways.

He practiced how to reach up, up, up

Until he did it with style and grace.

Puppet Pointers

1. Glue the pattern onto light-colored craft foam.

2. Outline details with a fine-tip permanent marker.

3. Glue on pieces of fabric for clothing. Trim the excess material.

3. Add wiggle eyes and yarn hair.

Stick Puppet Pattern

Directions: Color and cut out the puppet pattern.
Glue a craft-stick handle to the back. Use the puppet
as a storytelling prop.

uncle

Uu is for Uncle Utz

Learn-the-Alphabet Puppet Pals Scholastic Professional Books

 # Uncle Utz

uncle

Uncle Utz was a klutz. He was not unkind, unfriendly, or unhappy. He was just uncoordinated. No matter where he was, Uncle Utz was sure to bump into or break something.

Being clumsy upset Uncle Utz. One day, for the umpteenth time, he tripped and upset Aunt Una's teacup. "That's it!" he announced. "I don't understand why I'm so clumsy, but I'm going to do something about it!"

So Uncle Utz enrolled in a dance class. *Now I'll become graceful*, he thought.

In class, the students reached up, up, up. They twisted over and under. They balanced on one foot. Uncle Utz practiced in secret. He didn't show Aunt Una what he was learning.

Finally, the day of the dance recital arrived. Aunt Una sat in the front row. She was unusually worried. She was afraid that Uncle Utz would dance like a klutz.

When the curtain rose, the dancers pranced onto the stage. Aunt Una was surprised by what she saw. Uncle Utz was dressed as a butterfly. For the dance, he uncoiled his butterfly wings and bent and unbent his butterfly legs. In the finale, Uncle Utz danced while balancing a teacup on the tip of an umbrella. Uncle Utz was the most graceful dancer on the stage! Everyone applauded.

Nowadays, Uncle Utz is not nearly the klutz he used to be. And if he does suddenly become a klutz, Aunt Una just hums a tune. Uncle Utz instantly starts to dance and becomes graceful once again.

Practice Printing

uncle

Name

Vincent B. Vuddled

Vincent

Read-Aloud Puppet Story

Setting the Stage: Ask children to share any experiences with receiving a mysterious package in the mail. Were they able to guess what was in the package before they opened it? After sharing, tell students that they will hear a story about a man who receives a mysterious object in the mail.

Pocket-Chart Poem

Building Reading Skills: Print each line of the poem on a sentence strip. Place strips into a pocket chart. After reciting the poem several times, ask children what other words could substitute for violin (*vacuum cleaner, vegetable pot,* and so on). Print these variations on separate sentence-strip segments cut to fit over the original words. Have children take turns inserting the word cards into the pocket chart and then reading aloud the new versions.

Extension Activities

Stick Puppet Drama: Invite children to use their stick puppets to act out Vincent B. Vuddled's feelings and actions as they occur in the story. Afterward, have children demonstrate the different ways they moved their puppets to show Vincent receiving the violin, Vincent using the violin as a vase, a vacuum cleaner, and a vegetable pot, and Vincent talking to Ms. Velvet.

Read the story again so children have a chance to try out the different movements demonstrated.

Listen for V: Explain to children that Vincent's name begins with the sound of *v*. Say his name several times to reinforce the sound. Then have children hold their puppets in their laps as you reread the story. When they hear a word beginning with the *v* sound, have students draw a *v* in the air with their puppets. Record the identified *v* words on a chart or your alphabet word wall. As an extension, ask students to name resources in which they might find a list of *v* words. Possible responses might include a dictionary, encyclopedia, glossary, index, alphabet book, or phone book. Have children use some of these resources to find additional *v* words to add to your list.

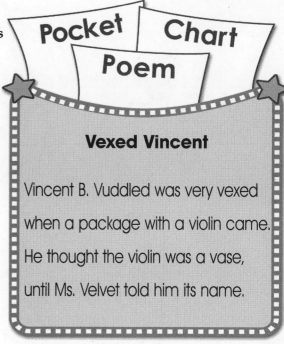

Pocket Chart Poem

Vexed Vincent

Vincent B. Vuddled was very vexed

when a package with a violin came.

He thought the violin was a vase,

until Ms. Velvet told him its name.

Puppet Pointers

1. Glue on pieces of fabric for clothing. Trim the excess material.

2. Add other details with a fine-tip permanent marker.

3. Add wiggle eyes and yarn hair.

4. Cut a bouquet from green craft foam. Glue small dried or silk flowers onto the bouquet. Use the bouquet as a prop.

Stick Puppet Pattern

Directions: Color and cut out the puppet pattern.
Glue a craft-stick handle to the back. Use the puppet
as a storytelling prop.

Vincent

Vv is for Vincent B. Vuddled

Vincent B. Vuddled

One day a package arrived at Mr. Vincent B. Vuddled's door. In it was a mysterious wooden object with a long handle, strings, and a hole in the center. Vincent was vexed. What was this strange object?

It has a hole in it, thought Vincent. *Maybe it's a vase*. He put some violets in the hole and set the vase on the table. Then he stepped back to look at it. He was still vexed.

It has a long handle, thought Vincent. *Maybe it's a vacuum cleaner*. He removed the violets and tried to clean the carpet with the strange object. It didn't work. Vincent was still vexed.

Maybe it's a vegetable pot, thought Vincent, looking at the handle and hole. He was just about to put water in the object when the doorbell rang. It was his neighbor, Ms. Velvet.

"Hello, Vincent!" sang Ms. Velvet, "Thank you so much for accepting delivery for my new violin."

"Violin?" said Vincent.

"Oh, Vincent, how silly to pretend that you don't know you're holding a violin!" gushed Ms. Velvet. "Please come over for dinner tonight so I can repay your favor!"

"Well, I was going to cook some vegetables, but I would rather have dinner with you," said Vincent as he handed Ms. Velvet the violin.

That night Vincent gave Ms. Velvet some violets. She put them in a glass vase. Then Ms. Velvet served Vincent a wonderful vegetable stew. And after dinner, she played a very nice tune on her new violin.

Practice Printing

Vincent

Name

V V V V V V V V V V V V

V V

V V

V V V V V V V V V V V V

V V

V V

V V V V V V V V V V V V

V v V v V v V v V v V v V v

V v V v

V v V v

Wolfy Wolf

wolf

Read-Aloud Puppet Story

Setting the Stage: Discuss the meaning of greed with children. Then tell them that they will hear a story about a wolf whose greed makes him look foolish.

Pocket-Chart Poem

Building Reading Skills: Print each line of the poem on a sentence strip. Place strips into a pocket chart. After reciting the poem several times, ask children what other words could substitute for weed the garden (*walk the dog, wash the dishes, fix the window,* and so on). Print these variations on separate sentence-strip segments cut to fit over the original words. Have children take turns inserting the word cards into the pocket chart and then reading aloud the new versions.

Extension Activities

Stick Puppet Drama: Invite children to use their stick puppets to act out Wolfy Wolf's feelings and actions as they occur in the story. Afterward, have children demonstrate the different ways they moved their puppets to show Wolfy looking for food, Wolfy knocking on the door, Wolfy eating the pie, Wolfy running away, and finally, the pie falling on top of Wolfy. (Tip: Have children make a puppet to represent the woman in the story. Also, children can use their free hands to represent the pie falling on Wolfy's head.)

Read the story again so children have a chance to try out the different movements demonstrated.

Words That Wow! Explain to children that Wolfy Wolf's name begins with the sound for *w.* Say his name several times to reinforce the sound. Then remind children that the smell of the watermelon pie made Wolfy Wolf say, "Wow!" Ask them to brainstorm a list of words beginning with *w* that make them say, "Wow!" Record the words on your alphabet word wall. (You might have children look at the *w* section in a dictionary for inspiration.) To extend, have students list words that begin with other letters. Add these lists to your word wall.

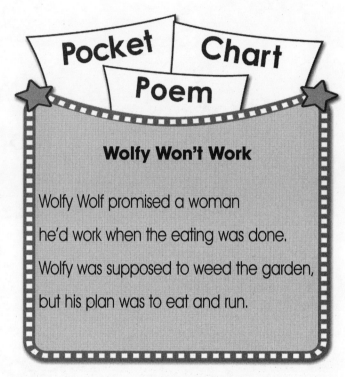

Pocket Chart Poem

Wolfy Won't Work

Wolfy Wolf promised a woman

he'd work when the eating was done.

Wolfy was supposed to weed the garden,

but his plan was to eat and run.

Puppet Pointers

1. Glue craft fur or terry cloth to the wolf shape. Trim the excess material.

2. Add additional details with a fine-tip permanent marker.

3. Glue on wiggle eyes.

4. Glue a craft-stick handle to the back.

5. Cut out two pie shapes from brown or tan craft foam. Use red puff paint to decorate the pieces to resemble watermelon pie.

Stick Puppet Pattern

Directions: Color and cut out the puppet pattern. Glue a craft-stick handle to the back. Use the puppet as a storytelling prop.

wolf

Ww is for Wolfy Wolf

Wolfy Wolf

wolf

Wolfy Wolf was hungry. He set out to look for food. He followed his nose until he came to a small cottage. In the window sat a warm watermelon pie. Wolfy's eyes widened and his mouth watered. "Wow!" he said. "I want that pie."

Wolfy knocked on the door. A woman answered. In a weak voice, Wolfy said, "I'm so hungry. May I have some of that watermelon pie in the window?"

"I'll share my pie, but you must work for it," said the woman. I want you to weed the garden, walk the dog, wash the dishes, and fix the window."

"After I eat some pie, I will work for you," said Wolfy. Secretly, he planned to eat, then run.

The watermelon pie was wonderful! Wolfy ate a wolf-sized piece. "Now it's time to work," said the woman as she placed the pie back in the window. But when she turned around, Wolfy was gone.

As Wolfy ran, he smelled the pie again. "Wow! I want more pie," he said. So he came back and crouched under the window. Just as he reached for the pie, the window slammed shut. *Wham!* The pie landed on Wolfy's head.

The woman rushed out and found Wolfy dripping with pie. "Wolfy! I thought you ran away, but I was wrong," she said with amusement. "You just wanted to surprise me by fixing that stuck window! Well, you're a wonderful worker. Too bad there's no more watermelon pie to pay you with!"

Practice Printing

wolf

Name

W W W W W W W W W

W W

W W

w w w w w w w w w w

w w

w w

W w W w W w W w W w W w

W w W w

W w W w

Mixed-Up Dr. X

Read-Aloud Puppet Story

Setting the Stage: Invite children to share their experiences about rushing to finish a task. Did being in a hurry cause them to make mistakes? After discussing, tell students that they will hear a story about a doctor who gets in a rush and mixes things up.

Pocket-Chart Poem

Building Reading Skills: Print each line of the poem on a sentence strip. Place strips into a pocket chart. After reciting the poem several times, ask children what other words could substitute for Giraffe (*Chicken, Turtle,* and so on). Print these variations on separate sentence-strip segments cut to fit over the original words. Have children take turns inserting the word cards into the pocket chart and then reading aloud the new versions.

Extension Activities

Stick Puppet Drama: Invite children to use their stick puppets to act out Dr. X's feelings and actions as they occur in the story. Afterward, have children demonstrate the different ways they moved their puppets to show Dr. X rushing and talking to patients. (Tip: Have children make puppets to represent the other characters in the story: Giraffe, Chicken, Snail, and Dr. Exact.)

Read the story again so children have a chance to try out the different movements demonstrated.

Listen for X: Explain to children that *Xray* begins with the sound for *x*. Say the word several times to reinforce the sound. Then have children hold their puppets in their laps as you reread the story. When they hear a word beginning with *x*, have children use their puppets to draw an *x* in the air. Then record the identified *x* words on chart paper. After reading the story, examine the list of words with students. With which letter do most of the words begin? *(e).* Tell children that although the words on the list begin with the *x* sound, they are actually spelled with a different first letter. Ask children to share ideas about why these words appear so often in this story.

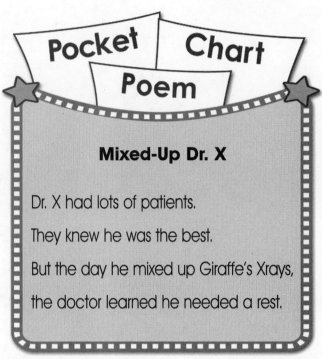

Pocket Chart Poem

Mixed-Up Dr. X

Dr. X had lots of patients.

They knew he was the best.

But the day he mixed up Giraffe's Xrays,

the doctor learned he needed a rest.

Puppet Pointers

1. Trace the pattern onto tan craft foam.

2. Add details with a fine-tip permanent marker.

3. Glue on craft feathers.

4. Glue on wiggle eyes.

Stick Puppet Pattern

Directions: Color and cut out the puppet pattern. Glue a craft-stick handle to the back. Use the puppet as a storytelling prop.

Dr. X

Xx is for Mixed-Up Dr. X

Mixed-Up Dr. X

Dr. X

Because he was the best doctor in town, Dr. X was always busy. Often, he had so many patients that he felt rushed. And when Dr. X was too tired and hurried, he would mix up things and make mistakes.

One afternoon, Dr. X was extremely busy. Giraffe came to him with an aching neck. Chicken came to him with a hurt beak. Snail told Dr. X that he had a sore shell. Dr. X carefully examined each patient and X-rayed each injury.

To Giraffe he said, "You have a cracked shell. Some shell glue is just the thing to fix you up."

"But, Doctor," said Giraffe, "that can't be right!"

To Chicken he said, "You have a pulled neck muscle. Some neck cream is just the thing to fix you up."

"But, Doctor," said Chicken, "that can't be right!"

To Snail he said, "You have an infected beak. Some beak pills will fix you up."

"But, Doctor," said Snail, "that can't be right!"

"Now, now, you three, don't worry," said Dr. X. "Just see Dr. Exact on your way out and she will give you your medicine. Good day, now!" Then he rushed off to his other patients.

On the way out, the three patients explained their problem to Dr. Exact. She realized exactly what went wrong. So she gave Giraffe the neck cream, Snail the shell glue, and Chicken the beak pills. Then Dr. Exact gave Dr. X the rest of the week off so he could relax.

Practice Printing

Dr. X

Name

X X X X X X X X X X X

X X

X X

X X X X X X X X X X X

X X

X X

X Xx X Xx X Xx X Xx X Xx X Xx X Xx

X Xx X Xx

X Xx X Xx

Yolanda Yak

yak

Read-Aloud Puppet Story

Setting the Stage: Ask children if they know someone who talks too much. Invite them to share their experiences with these "nonstop" talkers. Then tell students that they will hear a story about a yak who learns the value of talking less and listening more.

Pocket-Chart Poem

Building Reading Skills: Print each line of the poem on a sentence strip. Place strips into a pocket chart. After reciting the poem several times, ask children what other words could substitute for secret word (special sign, yellow bracelet, and so on). Print these variations on separate sentence-strip segments cut to fit over the original words. Have children take turns inserting the word cards into the pocket chart and then reading aloud the new versions.

Extension Activities

Stick Puppet Drama: Invite children to use their stick puppets to act out Yolanda Yak's feelings and actions as they occur in the story. Afterward, have children demonstrate the different ways they moved their puppets to show Yolanda talking, Yolanda yelping, and Yolanda listening. (Tip: Have each child use the Yolanda Yak pattern to make a Mr. Yogurt puppet.)

Read the story again so children have a chance to try out the different movements demonstrated.

Listen and Say Yes to Y: Explain to children that Yolanda Yak's name begins with the sound for y. Say her name several times to reinforce the sound. Then have children hold their puppets in their laps as you reread the story. When they hear a word beginning with y have children raise their puppets up and say "Yes!" Record the identified y words on your alphabet word wall or on chart paper. To extend, name one word at a time, some beginning with the y sound and some beginning with other sounds. If a word begins with y, ask children to raise their up puppets and say "Yes!" If the word begins with another sound, have children hold their puppets in their laps and say "No."

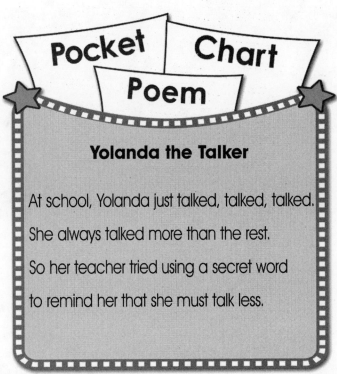

Pocket Chart Poem

Yolanda the Talker

At school, Yolanda just talked, talked, talked.

She always talked more than the rest.

So her teacher tried using a secret word

to remind her that she must talk less.

Puppet Pointers

1. Trace pattern onto tan craft foam.

2. Glue craft fur or terry cloth to the yak. Trim the excess material.

3. Add wiggle eyes and white (or yellow) horns cut from craft foam.

4. Glue a craft-stick handle to the back.

5. Tape on a yellow yarn bracelet to tell the story.

Stick Puppet Pattern

Directions: Color and cut out the puppet pattern. Glue a craft-stick handle to the back. Use the puppet as a storytelling prop.

yak

Yy is for
Yolanda Yak

Yolanda Yak

yak

Yolanda Yak loved to talk. She talked from the moment she woke up until she went to bed at night.

Her teacher, Mr. Yogurt, wanted Yolanda to talk less and listen more. "You have lots of good ideas to share, Yolanda," said Mr. Yogurt. "But, you must also *listen* to others' ideas." Yolanda knew this was true. She also knew that her classmates grew tired of all her yakkety-yakking.

To help, Mr. Yogurt whispered a secret word to Yolanda to remind her to talk less. But Yolanda was too busy talking to hear the secret word.

Mr. Yogurt made a sign that said, "Time to Listen!" He held up the sign as a signal for Yolanda to listen. But Yolanda was too busy yakking to read the sign.

Finally, Mr. Yogurt tied some yellow yarn around Yolanda's wrist. "What's this?" asked Yolanda. "It's a friendship bracelet," said Mr. Yogurt. "When I tug on it, you'll know it's time to stop talking and start listening."

The next time Yolanda was in class yakking away, she felt a little tug on her wrist. She nearly yelped. Then she realized that Mr. Yogurt had tugged on her yellow bracelet. So she stopped talking.

In time, Yolanda could remind herself to stop talking by tugging on her yarn bracelet. Because she became both a good talker and a good listener, Yolanda soon had many friends. And she finally understood why Mr. Yogurt called the yellow yarn a friendship bracelet!

Practice Printing

yak

Name

Y Y Y Y Y Y Y Y Y Y Y

Y Y

Y Y

y y y y y y y y y y y

y y

Y y

Y y Y y Y y Y y Y y Y y

Y y Y y

Y y Y y

Zippy Zebra

Read-Aloud Puppet Story

Setting the Stage: Ask children to describe their favorite recipes to cook. Then tell them that they will hear a story about a zebra's experience when he cooks soup for his family.

Pocket-Chart Poem

Building Reading Skills: Print each line of the poem on a sentence strip. Place strips into a pocket chart. After reciting the poem several times, ask children what other words could substitute for zucchini (*tomatoes, carrots, peppers, potatoes, lemon zest,* and so on). Print these variations on separate sentence-strip segments cut to fit over the original words. Have children take turns inserting the word cards into the pocket chart and then reading aloud the new versions. (If children are unfamiliar with lemon-zest—grated lemon rind—bring a lemon and a grater to school to demonstrate how to make lemon zest.)

Extension Activities

Stick Puppet Drama: Invite children to use their stick puppets to act out Zippy Zebra's feelings and actions as they occur in the story. Afterward, have children demonstrate the different ways they moved their puppets to show Zippy cooking, Zippy nodding, and Zippy talking to family members. (Tip: Have children each use the Zippy Zebra pattern to make the rest of the Zebra family puppets: Mother, Father, Sister, and Baby.)

Read the story again so children have a chance to try out the different movements demonstrated.

Listen for Z: Explain to children that Zippy Zebra's name begins with the sound for z. Say his name several times to reinforce the sound. Then have children hold their puppets in their laps as you reread the story. When they hear a word beginning with z, have students use their puppets to draw a z in the air. As children identify each z word, write it on chart paper or your alphabet word wall.

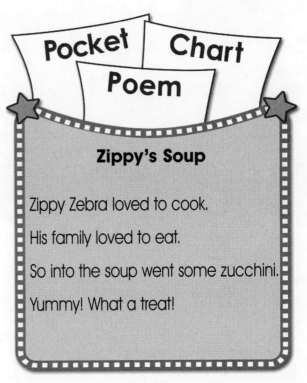

Pocket Chart Poem

Zippy's Soup

Zippy Zebra loved to cook.

His family loved to eat.

So into the soup went some zucchini.

Yummy! What a treat!

Puppet Pointers

1. Trace the zebra shape onto white craft foam.

2. Use a black permanent marker to fill in the zebra stripes.

3. Add other details with a fine-tip permanent marker.

4. Glue wiggle eyes on the zebra.

Stick Puppet Pattern

Directions: Color and cut out the puppet pattern.
Glue a craft-stick handle to the back. Use the puppet
as a storytelling prop.

Zz is for
Zippy Zebra

Zippy Zebra

Zippy Zebra decided to make his famous zucchini soup. He put a pot of water on the stove to boil. Then he sliced zucchini, diced tomatoes, cut up carrots and peppers, and quartered potatoes. He also grated some lemon zest.

While Zippy worked, Mother came into the kitchen. "I love your zucchini soup," she said. "But could you please leave out the tomatoes?" Zippy nodded.

Then Father came into the kitchen. "I love your zucchini soup," he said. "But could you please leave out the carrots and peppers?" Zippy nodded.

Later, Sister came into the kitchen. "I love your zucchini soup," she said. "But could you please leave out the potatoes?" Zippy nodded.

Finally, Baby came into the kitchen. "I love your zucchini soup," she said. "But could you please leave out the zucchini?" Zippy nodded and smiled to himself.

At dinner, Zippy served his family the soup. Mother looked into her bowl. Father, Sister, and Baby looked into their bowls, too.

"Where are the zucchini?" asked Mother.

"Where are the tomatoes?" asked Father.

"Where are the carrots and peppers?" asked Sister.

"Where are the potatoes?" asked Baby.

"Well, each of you asked me to leave something out," explained Zippy. "The lemon zest was all that was left to put in the soup. But I did put the foods that you didn't want into a pot of soup for myself. Would you like some?"

Everyone nodded.

After dinner, the whole Zebra family agreed that Zippy's zucchini soup was perfect with all the ingredients in it.

Practice Printing

zebra

Name

Z Z Z Z Z Z Z Z Z Z

Z Z

Z Z

Z Z Z Z Z Z Z Z Z Z

Z Z

Z Z

Zz Zz Zz Zz Zz Zz Zz Zz Zz Zz

Zz Zz

Zz Zz